Grammar
& Translation
Workbook

Tom Hockaday

How to use your Grammar & Translation Workbook

This workbook offers lots of support and practice to guide you through *Dynamo 3 French* (*Rouge* or *Vert*). It follows the content of both Pupil Books unit by unit – you'll recognise the same page titles!

Explanations to remind you of the key grammar points are followed by focussed grammar and translation exercises, which reuse vocabulary and themes from the matching units of the Pupil Books.

Vert or Rouge?

The swirl icon in the top right corners of the pages will tell you if a page is aimed at users of the *Vert* Pupil Book, the *Rouge* Pupil Book, or both:

There is also a Pupil Book page reference so that you can look back at that if you need to.

'Vert/Rouge' pages begin with exercises for pupils following the *Vert* course, then move on to questions for everyone (labelled *Vert/Rouge*) and finish off with some more tricky, *Rouge*-level tasks.

The exercise number icon shows you the level:

If you're following the *Vert* course, the *Rouge* exercises might practise grammar points that you haven't covered yet. But if you would like to try them, take a look at the grammar boxes first to help you.

End-of-module translation pages

At the end of each module, you'll find two pages full of translation practice. First, translation into English and then into French (e.g. pages 18–19).

You'll need to think about the grammar and vocabulary that you've learned throughout the module to answer these questions.

Module 5 – Grammaire

Module 5 of the Pupil Books is the grammar module, revisiting grammar from the whole book. Like the Pupil Books, the Workbook module is linked to francophone countries and people. Each unit begins with a quiz activity before a word search, code-breaker or crossword exercise.

Verb tables

The verb tables list key verbs in the different tenses that you use in *Dynamo 3*. Use these while completing the tasks, or to refer to any time you need.

Glossary

You can look up words from the Workbook in French or in English in the two-way glossary.

Tips

Look out for tip boxes to help you throughout the book:

Answers

Answers are included in the *Dynamo 3 Teacher's Guides* – just ask your teacher.

Published by Pearson Education Limited, 80 Strand, London, WC2R 0RL.

www.pearsonschoolsandfecolleges.co.uk

Text © Pearson Education Limited 2020

Developed by Lucy Loveluck
Edited by James Hodgson

Designed and typeset by Newgen KnowledgeWorks (P) Ltd, Chennai, India

Produced by Newgen Publishing UK

Original illustrations © Pearson Education Limited 2020
Illustrated by Beehive Illustration: Clive Goodyer, Andy Keylock, Gustavo Mazali, Martin Sanders, Matt Ward; KJA Artists: Mark, Neal, Sean; John Hallett; Andrew Hennessey; Alan Rowe

Picture research by Integra

Cover photo © Shutterstock: Sergii Molchenko

First published 2020

24
11

British Library Cataloguing in Publication Data
A catalogue record for this product is available from the British Library

ISBN 978 1 292 34656 4

Printed in the UK

Acknowledgements
We would like to thank Florence Bonneau, Pascale Collier, Liz Hammond, James Hodgson and Kate Mackinnon for their invaluable help in the development of this book.

The publisher acknowledges the use of the following:

Photographs: (Key: t–top; b–bottom; c–centre; l–left; r–right)

Dynamo banner: Sergii Molchenko/Shutterstock

Module 4: Shutterstock: Africa Studio 52cl, DrimaFilm 53bl.

Module 5: Getty Images: Stephane Cardinale – Corbis/Corbis Entertainment 77cr; Shutterstock: Julie Mayfeng 67cl, Lynne Cameron for The FA 73br, Firefighter Montreal 76bl.

Note from the publisher
Pearson has robust editorial processes, including answer and fact checks, to ensure the accuracy of the content in this publication, and every effort is made to ensure this publication is free of errors. We are, however, only human, and occasionally errors do occur. Pearson is not liable for any misunderstandings that arise as a result of errors in this publication, but it is our priority to ensure that the content is accurate. If you spot an error, please do contact us at resourcescorrections@pearson.com so we can make sure it is corrected.

Table des matières

Dynamo 3 © Pearson Education Ltd 2020

Point de départ

• Using *aimer* (etc.) + noun or infinitive

To talk about things that you like or dislike, use *aimer*, *adorer* or *détester* followed by a definite article (*le*, *la*, *l'*, *les*) and then a noun.

J'aime le judo.	I like judo.
J'adore la musique.	I love music.
Je n'aime pas l'EPS.	I don't like PE.
Je déteste les jeux vidéo.	I hate video games.

Unlike in English, you <u>must</u> include the definite article in French (the words in **bold** above).

 1 Circle the correct option each time.

1 I like **golf / tennis**. → *J'aime le golf.*

2 I love reading. → *J'aime / J'adore la lecture.*

3 I **don't like / hate** animals. → *Je déteste les animaux.*

4 I don't like the cinema. → *Je n'aime pas / déteste le cinéma.*

5 I love music. → *J'adore le / la musique.*

To talk about things that you like or dislike <u>doing</u>, use *aimer*, *adorer* or *détester* followed by a verb in the **infinitive** form.

J'adore faire du sport.	I love **to do** sport.
Je n'aime pas aller au cinéma.	I don't like **to go** to the cinema.

The infinitive verb can also be translated as **doing**, **going** etc.

Je déteste faire mes devoirs.   I hate **doing** my homework.

 2 Write out the jumbled sentences in the correct order.

1 | pas | jouer | je | tennis | n'aime | au |
Je n'aime pas jouer au tennis.
....

2 | faire | judo | du | j'aime |
....

3 | je | des | prendre | déteste | selfies |
....

4 | comédies | des | j'aime | regarder |
....

 3 Are the verbs followed by a noun or an infinitive? Write N or I.

1 J'adore le volleyball. **N**   3 Je n'aime pas aller en ville. ☐

2 Elle aime manger des pizzas. ☐   4 Il déteste le collège. ☐

4 Read the English sentences, then choose the words you need from the grid to translate them into French. Write three letters for each one.

		D	I	P
1	I don't like going to town at the weekend.	D	I	P
2	I like going cycling in the country.			
3	I really don't like PE at school.			
4	I love to play volleyball in the park.			
5	I hate sport, except rugby.			
6	I really like reading, especially comics.			

A	j'aime	G	la lecture	M	surtout les BD
B	j'aime beaucoup	H	l'EPS	N	dans le parc
C	j'adore	I	aller en ville	O	à la campagne
D	je n'aime pas	J	le sport	P	le weekend
E	je n'aime pas du tout	K	faire du vélo	Q	au collège
F	je déteste	L	jouer au volleyball	R	sauf le rugby

5 Jérémy from AdoDynamo magazine interviewed the Welsh popstar Llion, but then spilled coffee over the French translation. Can you help him out and fill in the blanks?

At the weekend,	Le weekend,
I like spending time	.... passer du temps
with my family.	avec ....
I really like	J'aime beaucoup
to go walking	.... des randonnées
in the countryside,	à la campagne,
but when it rains,	.... quand il pleut,
I like to go to the cinema.	j'aime .... au cinéma.
I love **popcorn**,	J'adore .... ,
however I hate **hotdogs**.	.... je déteste ....
On Sundays, I like to play tennis	Le .... , j'aime jouer au tennis
with my daughter Mia.	.... ma fille Mia.

'Popcorn' and 'hotdog' are the same in French and English. In French, both are masculine nouns. Remember to include the correct definite article (*le, la, l', les*) with nouns.

French sometimes uses the verb *faire* (to do) when English uses the verb 'to go':

faire du vélo → to go cycling

faire des randonnées → to go walking

Regular present tense –er verbs work like this:

chanter	(to sing)
je chante	I sing
tu chantes	you (singular) sing
il/elle/on chante	he/she sings / we sing
nous chantons	we sing
vous chantez	you (plural or polite) sing
ils/elles chantent	they sing

 1 Complete the endings of the regular –er verbs.

jouer (to play)

je jou......................

tu jou......................

il/elle/on jou......................

nous jou......................

vous jou......................

ils/elles jou......................

danser (to dance)

je dans......................

tu dans......................

il/elle/on dans......................

nous dans......................

vous dans......................

ils/elles dans......................

Some verbs are irregular and don't follow the same pattern:

aller (to go)   →   je **vais** (I go)

faire (to do)   →   je **fais** (I do)

être (to be)   →   je **suis** (I am)

 2 Separate out the words in the word snakes.

1   jejoueautennislelundi   ....

2   elledanseaprèslescours   ....

3   jefaisçaavecmonéquipe   ....

4   tujouesduviolonavecqui?   ....

5   nouschantonsàmidi   ....

Dynamo 3 © Pearson Education Ltd 2020

Negatives go around the verb:

Je ne chante pas.   I do **not** sing.

Je ne fais rien.   I do **nothing** / I don't do **anything**.

 3 Complete the missing words in the parallel sentences.

1	I don't play tennis every Wednesday.	.... au tennis tous les ....
2	Once a week, ... gymnastics.	Une fois par semaine, elle fait de la gymnastique.
3	Who do you play guitar with?	.... de la guitare avec qui?
4	I don't do anything	.... après les cours.

 4 Complete the verbs in the sentences and the crossword.

1 Je ne .... **(danser)** jamais avec mes amis.

2 Tu .... **(jouer)** au rugby avec ton équipe?

3 Ils .... **(danser)** avec qui?

4 Le mardi, vous .... **(manger)** à la cantine.

5 Elle .... **(jouer)** souvent au club de tennis.

6 À midi, nous .... **(jouer)** de la guitare.

7 Je .... **(être)** parfois amusant!

8 Nous .... **(chanter)** tous les soirs.

All of the verbs are regular *–er* verbs, except *être*. Can you remember the *je* form of *être*?

 5 Translate the sentences into French, using language from other exercises on this page to help you.

1 I play tennis with my brother.   ....

2 I go to dance club every Monday.   ....

3 I don't do anything after lessons.   ....

4 We don't dance at lunchtime.   ....

5 She **never** sings.   ....

6 Who do you play piano with?   ....

ne … jamais is the negative expression for 'never'.

Use *jouer **à*** with sports.   Most sports are masculine (*à + le* ⟶ *au*).

Use *jouer **de*** with instruments.   *Piano* is masculine (*de + le* ⟶ *du*).

Avoir (to have) and *être* (to be) are very important irregular verbs.

avoir	(to have)
j'ai	I have
tu as	you (singular) have
il/elle/on a	he/she has / we have
nous avons	we have
vous avez	you (plural or polite) have
ils/elles ont	they have

être	(to be)
je suis	I am
tu es	you (singular) are
il/elle/on est	he/she is / we are
nous sommes	we are
vous êtes	you (plural or polite) are
ils/elles sont	they are

 1 Write each verb phrase in the correct cloud.

j'ai	vous êtes
tu as	vous avez
il/elle/on est	tu es
je suis	nous sommes
il/elle/on a	ils/elles sont
ils/elles ont	nous avons

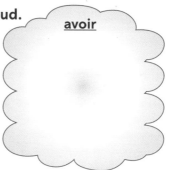

avoir

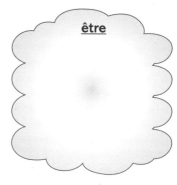

être

 2 Circle the correct part of *avoir* or *être* in each sentence.

1 Tu **a / as** des enfants?

2 Je ne **suis / est** pas petit.

3 Nous **avons / avez** les cheveux noirs.

4 Ils **sommes / sont** assez grands.

5 J' **ai / as** deux lapins.

6 Pascal **est / êtes** mon frère.

- -

 3 Cover up the top of the page. Write out the parts of *avoir* and *être* from memory. Then check how you did.

avoir

j' ▢▢

tu ▢▢

il/elle/on ▢

nous ▢▢▢▢▢

vous ▢▢▢▢

ils/elles ▢▢▢

être

je ▢▢▢▢

tu ▢▢

il/elle/on ▢▢▢

nous ▢▢▢▢▢▢

vous ▢▢▢▢

ils/elles ▢▢▢▢

2 Amis pour toujours!

• Using reflexive verbs

Reflexive verbs have a **reflexive pronoun** before the verb.

se disputer (avec)	to argue (with)
je **me** dispute	I argue
tu **te** disputes	you (singular) argue
il/elle/on **se** dispute	he/she argues / we argue
nous **nous** disputons	we argue
vous **vous** disputez	you (plural or polite) argue
ils/elles **se** disputent	they argue

me, *te* and *se* shorten to *m'*, *t'* and *s'* when the verb starts with a vowel or a silent 'h'.
je m'habille   I get dressed

G

1 Circle the correct reflexive pronoun for each sentence.

1	Je	me	m'	te	t'	se	s'	appelle Christophe.
2	Elle	me	m'	te	t'	se	s'	lève tard, le weekend.
3	Ils	me	m'	te	t'	se	s'	habillent à huit heures.
4	Tu	me	m'	te	t'	se	s'	disputes avec tes parents?
5	Aline	me	m'	te	t'	se	s'	fâche assez facilement.
6	Comment	me	m'	te	t'	se	s'	appelles-tu?

2 Unjumble the letters to rewrite the reflexive sentences correctly.

1   ej em ocuhde à etps ehuers   Je me douche à sept heures.

2   li es vale esl nsdet   ....

3   nuso suon diptsouns zseas ouvnste   ....

4   esell s'apntlplee Sraha te yAm   ....

5   ut t'eesdntn nibe acev est sparnet?   ....

3 Translate the sentences from exercise 2 into English.

| s'entendre | to get on |

1   ....

2   ....

3   ....

4   ....

5   ....

Think carefully about how to make each sentence sound natural in English. The word order may be very different. You may not need to include the reflexive pronoun in English.

The irregular verbs *avoir* (to have) and *être* (to be) are very useful for personal descriptions. **G**

avoir	(to have)
j'ai	I have
tu as	you (singular) have
il/elle/on a	he/she has / we have
nous avons	we have
vous avez	you (plural or polite) have
ils/elles ont	they have

être	(to be)
je suis	I am
tu es	you (singular) are
il/elle/on est	he/she is / we are
nous sommes	we are
vous êtes	you (plural or polite) are
ils/elles sont	they are

 1 Circle the five examples of *avoir* in this text, and underline the two examples of *être*.

Voici une photo de mon meilleur ami et moi. Moi, je suis très grand et j'ai les cheveux blonds.

Mon ami s'appelle Declan et il est assez petit. Il a les cheveux noirs et les yeux verts.

Moi, j'ai un frère, mais Declan, il a deux sœurs. Elles ont toutes les deux les cheveux roux.

Samuel

2 Write out the jumbled sentences in the correct order.

1 cheveux a les noirs elle   ....

2 ils bleus ont yeux les   ....

3 suis je grand assez   ....

4 très elle est petite   ....

5 roux cheveux avons les nous   ....

6 j'ai marron yeux les   ....

3 Translate the first three sentences from exercise 2 into English.

1 ....

2 ....

3 ....

4 Draw lines to make accurate sentences. There is more than one possible set of answers.

1	Elle	as	de temps en temps.
2	Je	nous disputons	avec ses parents.
3	Tu	ai	les cheveux mi-longs.
4	Nous	s'entend bien	tous les matins.
5	J'	se douche	de taille moyenne.
6	Il	suis	les yeux bleus.

> **G** Remember that reflexive verbs need a reflexive pronoun. See page 9.

 5 Jérémy's colleague has written an article full of mistakes. Circle the mistake in each verb and then write out those verbal phrases using correct spelling and grammar.

1 **Elle as** les yeux bleus et les cheveux noirs.   1 ....

2 **Je suis** les cheveux roux et les yeux bleus.   2 ....

3 **Il se fâchent** contre moi tous les jours.   3 ....

4 **Marc ne me dispute jamais** avec son frère.   4 ....

> **G** *Lui* and *elle* are often used with reflexive verbs to mean 'him' and 'her'.
>
> *Je me dispute avec **lui**.*   I argue with **him**.
> *Il se fâche contre **elle**.*   He gets angry with **her**.

6 This time, Jérémy's colleague has spilled chocolate milk on the notes from his interview with footballer Émilie Lefèvre. Can you fill in the missing words?

Jérémy: Est-ce que tu .... entends bien avec les autres joueurs?

Émilie: Oui, je m' .... très bien avec toute l'équipe. C' .... comme une grande famille – on .... dispute de temps en temps, bien sûr, mais j'aime bien l'équipe! Ma meilleure copine s' .... Alex. Elle .... les cheveux longs et blonds, comme une surfeuse! .... m'entends super-bien .... elle.

Jérémy: Quelle est ta routine journalière?

Émilie: Nous .... levons très tôt. .... me douche et je .... habille à six heures.

• Using the perfect tense

Use the perfect tense to say what you did or have done.
Most verbs use *avoir* to form the perfect tense, but some key verbs use *être*.
Remember the **1-2-3** rule:

1 subject pronoun (*je*, *tu*, *il/elle* etc.)

2 part of the verb *avoir* or *être* (known as the helping/auxiliary verb)

3 past participle

jouer (*avoir* as auxiliary verb)	
j'**ai** joué	I played
tu **as** joué	you played
il/elle/on **a** joué	he/she/we played
nous **avons** joué	we played
vous **avez** joué	you played
ils/elles **ont** joué	they played

aller (*être* as auxiliary verb)	
je **suis** allé(e)	I went
tu **es** allé(e)	you went
il/elle/on **est** allé(e)(s)	he/she/we went
nous **sommes** allé(e)s	we went
vous **êtes** allé(e)(s)	you went
ils/elles **sont** allé(e)s	they went

Past participles of regular verbs are easy to form:

–er verbs ⟶ *jouer* (to play) ⟶ *joué* (played)

–ir verbs ⟶ *finir* (to finish) ⟶ *fini* (finished)

–re verbs ⟶ *attendre* (to wait) ⟶ *attendu* (waited)

1 Draw lines to match up the English phrases with the correct words in French.

1	I played	j'	as	dansé
2	you (sing.) ate	il	avez	joué
3	he sang	vous	ai	regardé
4	they (f) listened	elles	a	écouté
5	you (pl) danced	tu	avons	mangé
6	we watched	nous	ont	chanté

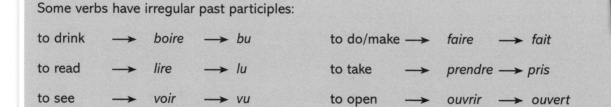

Some verbs have irregular past participles:

to drink ⟶ *boire* ⟶ *bu*   to do/make ⟶ *faire* ⟶ *fait*

to read ⟶ *lire* ⟶ *lu*   to take ⟶ *prendre* ⟶ *pris*

to see ⟶ *voir* ⟶ *vu*   to open ⟶ *ouvrir* ⟶ *ouvert*

to receive ⟶ *recevoir* ⟶ *reçu*

2 Separate out the word snakes into the 1-2-3 of the perfect tense.

1 J'aichanté ....

2 nousavonsjoué ....

3 jesuisallé ....

4 tuasvu ....

5 ilafait ....

6 noussommesallées ....

 Sandrine is speaking about her birthday. Write out the correct parts
of *avoir* or *être* and the past participles of the verbs given in brackets.

> Samedi dernier, c'était mon anniversaire. D'abord, j' ....ai retrouvé....
>
> (retrouver) mes amis au café. Nous .... (manger) des
>
> steak-frites et nous .... (boire) de la limonade.
>
> Après, je .... (aller) au centre commercial avec
>
> ma famille. Nous .... (faire) du bowling pendant
>
> deux heures. C'était trop marrant!

Pendant means 'during', but make your translation sound natural, not just a direct translation.

 Translate the second paragraph of the exercise 3 text into English.

....

....

5 Complete the missing parts of Marc's English–French parallel text. Take care to use the correct tense for each verb.

1	Last ...., it was my birthday.	Samedi dernier, c'était mon ....
2	Normally, I watch	Normalement, ... la télé.
3	But this ...., I went	Mais cette année, ...
4	to the cinema with	.... avec mes copains.
5	However, it was rubbish because	........................., c'était nul parce que
6	I didn't receive any presents!	.... de cadeaux!

You can use the near future tense to talk about future plans.
Use part of the verb *aller* (to go) + an infinitive:

je **vais** porter	I am going to wear
tu **vas** porter	you (singular) are going to wear
il/elle/on **va** porter	he/she is / we are going to wear
nous **allons** porter	we are going to wear
vous **allez** porter	you (plural or polite) are going to wear
ils/elles **vont** porter	they are going to wear

Remember the infinitive is the part of the verb you find in the dictionary and usually ends in –*er*, –*ir* or –*re*.

1   **Circle the correct part of *aller* in the sentences.**

1   Nous **allons** / **allez** manger des glaces.

2   Je **vas** / **vais** faire mes devoirs ce soir.

3   Ils **va** / **vont** porter l'uniforme scolaire.

4   Tu **vas** / **vais** sortir avec tes parents.

5   Vous **allons** / **allez** porter un costume gris.

6   Elle **va** / **vas** danser avec sa sœur.

2   **Draw lines to separate out the words, then write the sentences underneath.**

1   Cematinjevaisacheterunenouvellejupe.

2   Demainmatinilsvontchanterdanslachorale.

3   Samediprochainellevaporterdesbasketsblanches.

4   Leweekendprochainnousallonsmangerdelapizza.

1   ....

2   ....

3   ....

4   ....

3   **Unjumble the letters in the near future tense sentences.**

1   ej svai troper un anje lueb
    Je vais porter un jean bleu.

2   onus lalons troper sde setsetschau soirne
    ....

3   lele va merett uen ebor regou
    ....

4   je saiv tehcare nu aeouuvn talonpan risg
    ....

> In the near future tense, the negative goes around the part of *aller*:
>
> *Je **ne** vais **pas** regarder la télé.*   I am **not** going to watch TV.
> *Elle **ne** va **plus** porter de casquette.*   She is **no longer** going to wear a cap.
> *Ils **ne** vont **rien** acheter ce weekend.*   They are **not** going to buy **anything** this weekend.

4 **Rewrite the near future sentences in the correct order.**

1 | fleurs | acheter | ma | mère | va | des | pour | Elle |

Elle va acheter des fleurs pour ma mère.
....

2 | vont | Ils | rugby | plus | ne | jouer | dans | de | l'équipe |

....

3 | vais | aller | ne | en | Suisse | pas | Je |

....

4 | ensemble | Nous | sortir | allons | ce | weekend |

....

5 | ne | vas | cette | acheter | Tu | année | rien |

....

5 **Circle the correct spelling of the colour for each item of clothing.**

1   un pantalon **gris** / **grise**   4   un chapeau **vert** / **verts**

2   une chemise **rose** / **roses**   5   une robe **bleue** / **bleues**

3   des chaussures **blancs** / **blanches**   6   des baskets **noirs** / **noires**

> Remember that the adjective needs to agree with the noun in gender (m/f) and number (singular/plural).

6 **Complete the missing parts of the parallel sentences.**

1	J'adore ma robe	I love my green dress.
2	Elle est vraiment	.... really beautiful.
3	.... ma robe verte	I am going to wear my green dress
4	au restaurant .... soir.	to the restaurant tomorrow evening.
5	Nous n'allons pas manger de la pizza	.... pizza
6	car c'est .... ennuyeux.	because it's a bit boring.

Use the <u>present tense</u> to say what you normally do.

Use the <u>perfect tense</u> to say what you did (see pages 12–13).

present tense		perfect tense	
je joue	I play	j'ai joué	I played
je regarde	I watch	j'ai regardé	I watched
je fais	I do	j'ai fait	I did
je vais	I go	je suis allé(e)	I went

1 Write the verbs in the correct column.

j'ai mangé · je porte · j'ai attendu · j'ai cherché · j'achète · j'ai bu · je cherche · je mange · je bois · j'attends · j'ai porté · j'ai acheté

present tense	perfect tense
je mange	j'ai mangé

2 Translate the expressions into English and decide whether they would be used with a present or perfect tense verb. Circle the appropriate tense.

1   le weekend dernier   last weekend   present / (perfect)

2   normalement   ....   present / perfect

3   le weekend   ....   present / perfect

4   la semaine dernière   ....   present / perfect

5   en général   ....   present / perfect

6   hier   ....   present / perfect

3 Translate the paragraph into English on a separate sheet. Use the time/frequency expressions to help you choose the correct tense.

Normalement, au collège, je porte un pantalon noir et une chemise blanche.
Mais hier, j'ai porté un short vert et un pull jaune parce que c'était
mon anniversaire.
Le weekend, en général, je porte un jean bleu et des baskets rouges, mais le
weekend dernier, j'ai acheté un nouveau sweat à capuche marron.

Manu

c'était   it was

4 Qu'est-ce que tu vas porter?

• More near future tense

Pages 16–17

Use the near future tense to talk about future plans:

je **vais** porter	nous **allons** porter
tu **vas** porter	vous **allez** porter
il/elle/on **va** porter	ils/elles **vont** porter

1 Complete the parts of *aller* in the sentences.

1 Pour la fête, je .... porter un jean noir.

2 Pierre .... mettre un short et un tee-shirt.

3 Nous .... emprunter des cravates roses.

4 Tu .... porter ton uniforme scolaire?

5 Aline et Sarah .... acheter de nouvelles robes.

2 Complete the table to turn these present tense verbs into positive and negative near future tense verbs (using *ne ... pas*).

Change the verb into the infinitive form, put the correct part of *aller* in front of the infinitive, and then add *ne … pas* around the part of *aller*.

	positive present tense verb	positive near future tense verb	negative near future tense verb
1	je fais	je vais faire	je ne vais pas faire
2	elle porte		
3	nous écoutons		
4	je vais		

3 Now put these sentences into the negative near future tense using the steps from exercise 2 to help you.

1 Vous écoutez de la musique pop. ....

2 Ils achètent de nouveaux pantalons. ....

4 Translate the sentences into French.

1 We are going to eat at a restaurant because it's **my mum's birthday**.

Word order will be 'the birthday of my mum'.

....

2 You (plural or polite) are going **to go** cycling with Michel next weekend.

Use *faire* not *aller*.

....

3 She is going to buy a **new blue dress** for the party.

'New' will go before the noun, and 'blue' after the noun – make sure they both agree with *robe* (f).

....

T

- The **word order** will sometimes be different between the French and English.
- You may need **more words** or **fewer words** in English than there are in French.
- Pay attention to **time phrases** and other clues. Use these to build your sentence in English.

VERT

1 Use the English words in the box to translate the sentences into English.

wearing	he	today	to	am	argue	I	town	last	weekend
with	I	new	often	quite	went	my	jumper	parents	my

1 Aujourd'hui, je porte mon nouveau pull. ....

2 Le weekend dernier, il est allé en ville. ....

3 Je me dispute assez souvent avec mes parents. ....

T

- Avoid translating word for word. Think about what the <u>whole sentence</u> means and how you would <u>make it sound natural</u> in English.

VERT
2
ROUGE

Translate the sentences into English.

1 Samedi dernier, j'ai fait du vélo avec mes amis.
Last Saturday, ...

2 Normalement, je porte un tee-shirt bleu et des baskets noires.

....

3 Parfois, je me dispute avec mon petit frère.

....

4 Elle adore nager et elle aime aussi aller au centre commercial.

....

3
ROUGE
Circle the two mistakes in each English sentence and then write out the correct English translation.

1 Tu chantes dans la chorale le lundi? ➜ Do you sing in(the bath) on(Tuesdays)?
Do you sing in the choir ... .

2 D'habitude, je porte un pantalon noir. ➜ Sometimes, I wear a black blazer.

....

3 Il se fâche souvent contre moi. ➜ She often argues with me.

....

Dynamo 3 © Pearson Education Ltd 2020

> • Check your **verb** is in the correct **tense** and matches the **subject** (person doing the verb).
> • Reflexive verbs – remember to include the **reflexive pronoun** in French.

VERT 1 Unjumble the French words to translate the English sentences.

1	We dance after classes.	après les dansons nous cours	Nous dansons ...
2	I ate a delicious cake.	un mangé gâteau délicieux j'ai	....
3	I get up at 7am.	lève je à heures me sept	....
4	She argues with her sister.	sœur se dispute avec elle sa	....

VERT 2 ROUGE Translate the sentences into French. Use the boxes to check you have the correct number of words each time.

1	She		wears		blue shoes.		

2	He		argues	quite	often	with	my	brother.

3	I		didn't play		tennis		last weekend.	

4	I	am going	to go	to the	cinema	tomorrow	evening.

3 ROUGE Translate the text into French.

> Use *faire*, not *aller*.

Last Saturday, I went to Oxford with my family. We **went shopping**. My dad bought some trousers and I bought some white trainers. (I **never** wear shoes at the weekend!) Next weekend, I am going to watch some films with my friend James.

Aycha

> Use *ne … jamais*.

....

....

....

....

....

Point de départ

• *on peut* + infinitive

1 Find the French–English pairs of infinitive verbs and shade each pair in a different colour.

trouver	to earn	gagner	ranger
to look after	aider	to help	to think
to work	garder	penser	to find
laver	to wash	to tidy	travailler

The infinitive is the verb as you find it in the dictionary, e.g. *aider* (to help).

The present tense is used to talk about what you normally do or what you are doing at the moment. Regular *–er* verbs such as those above are used in the *je* form like this:

je gagne	I earn	*je lave*	I wash
je pense	I think	*je garde*	I look after

2 Underline the verb in the sentences. Does the sentence make sense? If not, explain why.

1 J'<u>aide</u> mon chat avec ses devoirs. _No – cats don't have any homework!_

2 Je gagne vingt euros par semaine. ....

3 Je range mon petit frère. ....

4 Je travaille dans un hôpital. ....

5 Je garde mon prof de maths. ....

The **modal verb** *pouvoir* means 'to be able to', but is often translated as 'can'. It's usually followed by another verb in the infinitive form.

On peut aider à la maison.	You can help at home.
On peut faire du baby-sitting.	You can do babysitting.

3 Choose the correct infinitive for each line in the table. Use the correct form of the verb for each column.

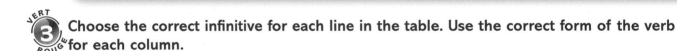

ranger   trouver   travailler   gagner   aider

	present tense *je* form	*on peut* + infinitive
1	Je travaille .... avec mes parents.	On peut travailler .... dans le jardin.
2	J'.......... à la maison.	On peut .... les voisins.
3	Je .... de l'argent.	On peut .... cent euros par mois.
4	Je .... ça difficile.	On peut .... un petit boulot.
5	Je .... ma chambre.	On peut .... la maison.

> *Pouvoir* and *devoir* are modal verbs that are usually followed by an infinitive. They are both irregular.
>
> | *pouvoir* | to be able to (can) |
> |---|---|
> | *je peux* | I can |
> | *on peut* | you/we can |
> | *nous pouvons* | we can |
>
> | *devoir* | to have to (must) |
> |---|---|
> | *je dois* | I must |
> | *on doit* | you/we must |
> | *nous devons* | we must |

G

4 **Draw lines to separate out the words, then write the English translations.**

1 ondoittrouverunpetitboulot ....

2 nouspouvonsfairedubaby-sitting ....

3 jedoisaiderdanslejardin ....

4 nousdevonsfairelacuisine ....

5 onpeutalleraumarché ....

5 **Underline all the English parts in this tangled text. Then rewrite the whole text in French underneath.**

> Use *pour* + infinitive.

In order to earn de l'argent, de temps en temps, I have to help mon père in the garden. It's assez facile, but un peu boring.

My sister et moi, nous devons aussi do the cooking et nourrir les animaux **every day**. In my opinion, c'est juste.

Le weekend, I can sortir with my friends, but I must rentrer avant nine o'clock du soir.

Eliot

t _ _ _ l _ _ j _ _ _ _

....

....

....

....

....

....

....

Qu'est-ce que tu veux faire ...?

• *vouloir* + infinitive

Vouloir (to want) is a modal verb.

je veux	I want
tu veux	you want
il/elle/on veut	he/she wants / we want
nous voulons	we want
vous voulez	you want
ils/elles veulent	they want

It is followed by another verb in the <u>infinitive</u> form.

Je veux <u>aller</u> au cinéma.   **I want <u>to go</u> to the cinema.**

---

 1 Complete the sentences with the correct form of the verb *vouloir*.

1 Je .... être danseur.

2 Elle .... être policière.

3 Tu .... être actrice?

4 Nous .... travailler dans un hôpital.

5 Elles .... gagner beaucoup d'argent.

6 Il .... être mécanicien.

Lots of job nouns have both masculine and feminine forms in French.

---

 2 Circle the correct form of the job noun (masculine or feminine) and then translate the sentence into English.

 1 Il veut être (danseur) / danseuse.

He wants to be a dancer.

 2 Elle veut être **infirmier / infirmière**.

....

 3 Je (m) veux être **policier / policière**.

....

 4 Elle veut être **mécanicien / mécanicienne**.

....

 5 Je (f) veux être **ingénieur / ingénieure**.

....

6 Il veut être **acteur / actrice**.

....

3 Write out the jumbled sentences in the correct order.

1   je car intéressant infirmière veux être c'est

Je veux être infirmière car c'est intéressant.

2   musicienne veux fatigant pas je ne car être c'est

Je ne veux pas ...

3   c'est veut elle être passionnant danseuse car

4   il être veut c'est pas ne car dangereux pilote

5   car je être c'est professeur veux varié

4 Translate the sentences into French.

> Remember, you don't need to say *un/une* before the job as you would in English.

1   I want to be a police officer because it's exciting.

2   She wants to be a **scientist** because it's important. | scientifique |

3   He wants to be a nurse because it's varied.

4   I don't want to be a teacher because it's tiring.

5 Use the words in the table to translate the text into French.

un jour	au lycée	travailler	j'aime	aller	j'adore
pour	vétérinaire	les animaux	de 16 ans	aider	être
je peux	à l'âge	les autres	je veux	étudier	et
les sciences	aussi	car	beaucoup	je veux	en équipe

At the age of 16, I want to go to sixth form college to study science, because I want to be a vet one day. I love animals and I can work in a team as well. I really like helping others.   **Albane**

The **near future tense** is used to talk about what **is going to happen** in the future. Use the verb *aller* (to go) + the infinitive.

je **vais** habiter	I am going to live
tu **vas** habiter	you are going to live
il/elle/on **va** habiter	he/she is / we are going to live
nous **allons** habiter	we are going to live
vous **allez** habiter	you are going to live
ils/elles **vont** habiter	they are going to live

 Circle the correct form of the verb *aller* in the sentences.

1 Je **vais** / **vas** regarder un film.

2 Vous **allons** / **allez** jouer au foot.

3 Ils **va** / **vont** acheter une maison.

4 Elle **va** / **vas** voyager en Espagne.

5 Nous **vont** / **allons** habiter en ville.

6 Tu **vais** / **vas** être riche.

 Draw lines to form sentences that make sense.

1 Je vais acheter
2 Elle va habiter
3 Nous allons avoir
4 Ils vont jouer
5 Tu vas manger
6 Vous allez regarder

a un film à la télé.
b en France.
c au restaurant.
d une nouvelle voiture.
e deux enfants.
f au tennis ce soir.

ne ... pas forms a sandwich around *aller* to make the verb negative.

*Je **ne** vais **pas** avoir d'enfants.*   I am **not** going to have children.

3 Translate the near future tense sentences into English.

1 Je ne vais pas habiter en France.   I am not going to ....

2 Elle ne va pas jouer aux cartes.   She is not ....

3 Nous n'allons pas avoir d'enfants.   ....

4 Ils ne vont pas être riches.   ....

5 Tu ne vas pas aller en ville.   ....

4 Jérémy the terrible journalist accidentally shredded his interview with Madagascan singer Rudy. Write out the full paragraph in the correct order.

1 être riche et célèbre. Dans dix

2 bénévole. Je vais avoir une grande

3 Je m'appelle Rudy et je suis

4 ans, je vais faire du travail

5 d'enfants. Ce sera génial.

6 je vais habiter à Paris et je vais

7 chanteur et danseur. À l'avenir,

8 maison, mais je ne vais pas avoir

Je m'appelle Rudy et je suis
....
....
....
....
....
....
....

Use all available clues to help you out, from your knowledge of the near future tense to any punctuation.

5 Translate the sentences into French.

1 In the future, I am going to live in Spain.
   À l'avenir, je vais habiter ...

2 In ten years, I am going **to do voluntary work**.
   Dans dix ans, je ...

   Use *faire du travail bénévole.*

3 In 25 years, she is going to live in New York.
   Dans vingt-cinq ans, ...

4 In the future, I am going to have three children.
   ....

5 In ten years, I am going to be famous.
   ....

6 In 25 years, you are going to buy a house.
   ....

Use the future tense to talk about what **will happen**.
For regular –er and –ir verbs, use the infinitive as the future stem and add these endings:

> je travailler**ai**
> tu travailler**as**
> il/elle/on travailler**a**
> nous travailler**ons**
> vous travailler**ez**
> ils/elles travailler**ont**

Other verbs use the same endings but have their own future stem:

–re verbs (e.g. attendre)	⟶	attendr-	⟶	j'attend**rai** (I will wait)
avoir	⟶	aur-	⟶	j'aur**ai** (I will have)
être	⟶	ser-	⟶	je ser**ai** (I will be)
aller	⟶	ir-	⟶	j'ir**ai** (I will go)
faire	⟶	fer-	⟶	je fer**ai** (I will do)

1 **Complete the future tense verbs with the correct ending: -ai or -as.**

1 À l'avenir, j'aur.................. trois enfants.

2 D'ici cinq ans, tu habiter.................. aux États-Unis.

3 Est-ce que tu fer.................. du snowboard?

4 Je n'habiter.................. pas à l'étranger.

5 D'ici dix ans, je travailler.................. chez Facebook.

6 À l'avenir, tu ser.................. très célèbre!

2 **Choose from the verbs in the box to complete each sentence so that it makes sense in the future tense.**

1 L'année prochaine, je .... du travail bénévole.

2 Ensuite, j' .... une voiture.

3 Dans deux ans, j' .... à l'université.

4 D'ici cinq ans, je .... dans une banque.

5 J' .... une grande maison avec une piscine.

6 D'ici vingt ans, je .... riche.

7 J' .... trois enfants. Ce sera chouette.

8 Et toi, qu'est-ce que tu .... à l'avenir?

irai
ferai
feras
achèterai
aurai
travaillerai
aurai
serai

3 Write out the jumbled sentences in the correct order and then translate them into English.

1

> ~~à l'avenir~~ avec
> en ~~j'habiterai~~ ma
> famille France

1 À l'avenir, j'habiterai …

In the future, I will live …

2

> dans Ferrari ans
> dix une j'aurai rouge

2 ....

....

3

> je un très heureuse
> serai car petit copain
> j'aurai sympa

3 ....

....

....

4

> serai pas d'enfants je
> marié mais je n'aurai

4 ....

....

4 What tense are these sentences in? Tick the correct column.

		present	perfect	near future	future
1	Je serai riche et célèbre.				
2	Tu as fait du travail bénévole?				
3	Tu vas acheter une voiture bleue.				
4	J'ai travaillé chez Google.				
5	Je vais aller en Chine.				
6	Tu auras quatre enfants.				
7	Tu as des frères et sœurs?				

5 Underline all the English parts in this tangled text. Then rewrite the whole text in French underneath.

L'année prochaine, I will go to Spain with my family. Ce sera fantastique. I will travel by car et by boat, et je logerai dans un grand hôtel de luxe. Il y aura a large swimming pool and il fera always beau. Je ne travaillerai pas but tous les jours, I will go du karting.

....

....

....

....

....

....

loger to stay

3 Au travail, les robots!

• Using the perfect tense with *ne ... pas*

G

Use the perfect tense to say what you did in the past. (See page 12 for more help.)
To make a perfect tense verb negative, put **ne ... pas** around the part of *avoir* or *être*.

j'ai regardé	I watched	→	*je n'ai **pas** regardé*	I **didn't** watch
j'ai joué	I played	→	*je n'ai **pas** joué*	I **didn't** play
je suis allé(e)	I went	→	*je **ne** suis **pas** allé(e)*	I **didn't** go

1 Add *ne ... pas* to make the verbs negative, then translate them into English.
Remember that *ne* shortens to *n'* before a vowel!

1 Je .... ai .... travaillé dans le jardin. ....

2 Je .... ai .... gardé les enfants. ....

3 Je .... suis .... allée au supermarché. ....

4 Je .... ai .... fait la vaisselle. ....

5 Je .... suis .... allé en ville. ....

2 Rewrite the positive perfect tense sentences as negatives.

1 Ce matin, j'ai aidé à la maison. *Ce matin, je n'ai pas aidé à la maison.*

2 Hier, j'ai préparé les repas. ....

3 Lundi dernier, j'ai rangé les chambres. ....

4 Hier soir, je suis allé au parc. ....

3 Complete the missing parts of the parallel translation. | *faire le café to make the coffee* |

La semaine dernière, ... au collège.	Last ...., I helped at school.
D'abord, ... le café pour les profs.	Firstly, I made the coffee ....
Après, j'ai servi les repas à la cantine.	Then, ... meals in the canteen.
Cependant, ... les salles de classe	............................, I didn't tidy the classrooms,
et .... la vaisselle.	and I didn't do the washing-up.
L'après-midi, je ne suis pas allé à la piscine.	In the afternoon, ... to the swimming pool.
C'était très ennuyeux.	It was............................

On is used to mean '<u>we</u>' or '<u>people</u>'. The future tense ending for *on* is *-a*:

on mangera	we/people will eat
on ira	we/people will go

The future tense of *c'est* is *ce sera* (it will be).
The future tense of *il y a* is *il y aura* (there will be).

See page 26 to remind yourself how the future tense is formed.

1 Are the verbs in these sentences in the present tense (*maintenant*) or the future tense (*à l'avenir*)? Tick the correct column.

	maintenant	à l'avenir
1 On fera des livraisons avec des drones.	☐	☐
2 On achète presque tout en ligne.	☐	☐
3 On ne mangera plus de viande.	☐	☐
4 On portera des vêtements intelligents.	☐	☐
5 On voyage en avion électrique.	☐	☐
6 On a des collèges virtuels.	☐	☐

la viande meat
presque almost

2 Separate out the word snakes to make future tense sentences.

1 àl'avenirilyauraunrobotdanschaquemaison

....

2 àl'avenironvoyageraenavionsanspilote

....

3 dansvingtansonhabiterasurlaLune

....

4 d'icitrenteansceseratrèseffrayant

....

3 Translate the text into French on a separate sheet, using the language on this page to help you.

In the future, the world will be very different.

We will live on the moon and there will be **pilotless** planes.

People will **no longer** eat meat and there will be a robot in every **room**.

It will be incredible.

Use *sans* …

la pièce = room

Use the negative *ne … plus*.

> **G**
>
> The **present tense** is made up of a subject pronoun + conjugated verb. E.g:
>
> j'ai   je suis   je fais   je vais   j'habite
>
> The **near future tense** is made up of a subject pronoun, the correct present tense form of *aller* and an infinitive. E.g:
>
> je vais avoir   je vais être   je vais faire   je vais aller   je vais habiter

 1 Write the correct French infinitive under the English.

> garder   acheter   être   adorer   vendre   aller
> écrire   avoir   habiter   gagner   faire   poster

The infinitives will be in alphabetical order in French!

 to buy
....

 to love
....

 to go
....

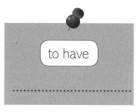 to have
....

 to write
....

 to be
....

 to do/make
....

 to earn/win
....

 to look after
....

 to live
....

 to post (online)
....

 to sell
....

 2 Translate the time expressions into English and then circle 'present' or 'future'.

1	à l'avenir	_in the future_	present / (future)
2	en ce moment	....	present / future
3	tous les jours	....	present / future
4	demain soir	....	present / future
5	le weekend	....	present / future
6	le weekend prochain	....	present / future

3 Draw lines to match up the questions and answers.

1 Qu'est-ce que tu fais pour gagner de l'argent?

2 Qu'est-ce que tu vas faire demain soir?

3 Qu'est-ce que tu vas faire à l'avenir?

4 Qu'est-ce que tu postes en ligne?

a Je vais garder mon petit frère.

b Je poste souvent des photos de mes amis.

c Je vends de l'eau aux touristes.

d Je vais habiter en France avec mon père.

4 Use the time expression to help you circle the correct verb in each sentence.

1 Demain soir, **je regarde / je vais regarder** un film à la télé.

2 Tous les jours, **je vais / je vais aller** au collège avec mes amis.

3 À l'avenir, **je suis / je vais être** assez riche.

4 En ce moment, **j'adore / je vais adorer** les milkshakes à la fraise.

5 Choose and shade a box from each column to translate the sentences from exercise 4. Use a different colour for each sentence.

1 Tomorrow night,	I go	strawberry	on TV.
2 Every day,	I am going to be	a film	rich.
3 In the future,	I am going to watch	quite	with my friends.
4 At the moment,	I love	to school	milkshakes.

6 Rewrite the French sentences below in full to translate the English sentences.

1 Every day, I do the washing-up with my parents.

Tous les jours, je fais la vaisselle avec mes parents.

....

2 In the future, I am going to live in a big apartment.

À l'avenir, je vais habiter dans un grand appartement.

....

3 At the moment, I am writing lots of posts for my website.

En ce moment, j'écris beaucoup de postes pour mon site web.

....

4 Tomorrow evening, I am going to buy a new skirt.

Demain soir, je vais acheter une nouvelle jupe.

....

G

perfect (past) tense	present tense	future tense
(avoir/être + past participle)	(conjugated verb)	(stem + future ending)
j'ai travaillé	je travaille	je travaillerai
tu as inventé	tu inventes	tu inventeras
il/elle/on est arrivé(e)(s)	il/elle/on arrive	il/elle/on arrivera
nous avons joué	nous jouons	nous jouerons
vous avez mangé	vous mangez	vous mangerez
ils/elles ont aimé	ils/elles aiment	ils/elles aimeront

Use **est-ce que** to form questions in all three tenses.
Use a question word + *est-ce que* + subject pronoun + conjugated verb:

Pourquoi **est-ce que** tu as créé le robot?   Why did you create the robot?

1 Unjumble the question words.
ROUGE

1 (who)   uiq   ....   4 (what)   qeu   ....

2 (when)   anduq   ....   5 (why)   prooiuqu   ....

3 (where)   ùo   ....

2 Are these questions in the past, present or future tense? Underline the verb and then
ROUGE tick the correct column.

		past	present	future
1	Où est-ce que tu travailles en ce moment?			
2	Pourquoi est-ce qu'elle a immigré en France?			
3	Quand est-ce que tu joueras au golf?			
4	Avec qui est-ce qu'il a fait ses devoirs?			
5	Qu'est-ce que tu aimes comme musique?			
6	Où est-ce qu'il mangera demain soir?			

3 Circle the correct question word needed each time, then translate the questions into English.
ROUGE

1   **Pourquoi / Qui** est-ce que tu iras aux États-Unis?

....

2   **Quand / Où** est-ce qu'elle habite en ce moment?

....

3   **Qui / Qu'** est-ce que je mangerai ce soir?

....

4   **Quand / Qui** est-ce que tu rentreras chez toi?

....

4 Rewrite the *tu* questions as *il, elle, ils* or *elles* questions as specified in the brackets.

> Think carefully about how the verb will need to change to match up with the new subject.

1 Qu'est-ce que tu as inventé récemment? (elle)

   Qu'est-ce qu'elle a inventé récemment? ....

2 Qu'est-ce que tu fais comme métier? (il)

   ....

3 Pourquoi est-ce que tu as créé cette voiture? (ils)

   ....

4 Avec qui est-ce que tu iras au Mexique? (elle)

   ....

5 Quand est-ce que tu gagneras le prix? (elles)

   ....

6 Où est-ce que tu étudies les sciences? (ils)

   ....

5 Can you make an accurate question out of each collection of words? What tense is the question in?

1

choisi voiture as ~~que~~ la tu ~~pourquoi~~ ~~est-ce~~ verte

Pourquoi est-ce que ... .

....

past ✓ present ☐ future ☐

2

que vacances où les passes d'habitude est-ce tu

....

....

past ☐ present ☐ future ☐

3

vous à travaillerez est-ce quand que Londres

....

....

past ☐ present ☐ future ☐

4

la pas est-ce tu lecture aimes pourquoi que n'

....

....

past ☐ present ☐ future ☐

1 Choose and shade a box from each column to translate the sentences into English.
Use a different colour for each sentence.

1 Je veux être professeur.

2 On peut faire du baby-sitting.

3 Elle va travailler dans un café.

4 Je n'ai pas regardé le film.

I	didn't	to work	the film
she	want	to be	babysitting
you	is going	watch	in a café
I	can	do	a teacher

2 Circle the three perfect tense verbs and underline the three near future tense verbs in this text about RoboDynamo. Then write them out underneath in both French and English.

Bonjour! Je m'appelle RoboDynamo et je travaille dans le bureau du magazine AdoDynamo, avec Jérémy. La semaine dernière, j'ai aidé Jérémy avec trois articles pour le magazine et j'ai préparé les repas à la cantine. Cependant, je n'ai pas fait la vaisselle! Demain, je vais ranger le bureau et je vais prendre des photos pour le magazine. Jérémy va être très content de moi!

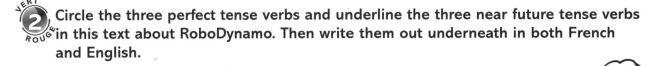

perfect tense		near future tense	
1 ...... j'ai aidé	...... I helped	1	....
2	....	2	....
3	....	3	....

Keep an eye out for **cognates** or **near cognates** as you might be able to work out what they mean in English, even if you've never seen the French word before.

3 Complete the translation of the interview into English.

A: Laurent, qu'est-ce que tu fais pour gagner de l'argent?

B: Le weekend, je garde mon petit frère et je fais toujours la vaisselle pour mes parents.

A: Et quels sont tes projets pour l'avenir?

B: Dans quatre ans, j'irai à l'université, et d'ici dix ans, je travaillerai à Paris.

A: Laurent, ...
.... money?

B: At the weekend, ...
....
.... parents.

A: And .... future?

B: ....
....
.... Paris.

> Read the English carefully to make sure you have identified **which tense** needs to be used in French.

1 Use the first letter of each word to help translate the phrases into French.

1 You can earn money.

2 I tidy my bedroom.

3 I am going to live abroad.

4 I went to the market.

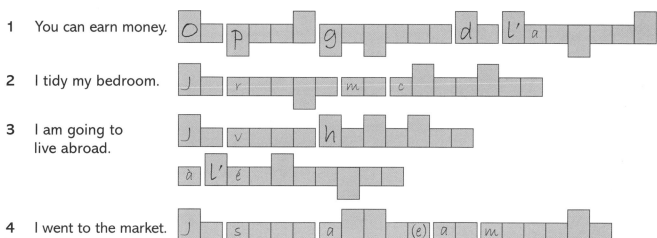

Which is the correct translation? Circle A or B.

1	She went to town.	A	Elle est allée en ville.	B	Elle va aller en ville.
2	I am not going to buy …	A	Je ne vais pas avoir …	B	Je ne vais pas acheter …
3	Where did he study?	A	Où est-ce qu'il a étudié?	B	Quand est-ce qu'il a étudié?
4	It will be very cool.	A	Ce sera très cool.	B	C'était très cool.
5	You can help the neighbours.	A	On doit aider les voisins.	B	On peut aider les voisins.
6	I want to be a pilot.	A	Je voudrais être pilote.	B	Je veux être pilote.

> Be careful with words we miss out in English but which must be there in French, and vice versa.

3 Translate the sentences into French.

1 I (m) want to be a dancer because it's creative and varied.

....

2 **In order to earn** money, **you** can find a part-time job.　　　| Use *pour* + infinitive. |　| Use *on* for 'you'. |

....

3 She **will be** happy but she will not be famous.　　| One word in French – the future tense of *être*. |

....

4 Why did you create a new robot?

....

Point de départ

• Adjectives and direct object pronouns (*le, la, les*)

Adjectives must agree with the noun they are describing, in both **gender** (masculine or feminine) and **number** (singular or plural).

masculine singular	feminine singular	masculine plural	feminine plural
amusant	amusante	amusants	amusantes
intéressant	intéressante	intéressants	intéressantes
démodé	démodée	démodés	démodées
bon	bonne	bons	bonnes
nul	nulle	nuls	nulles
ennuyeux	ennuyeuse	ennuyeux	ennuyeuses

 1 Circle the correct spelling of the adjective in each sentence.

> Remember *le* (m), *la* (f) and *les* (plural) all mean 'the' in English.

1 Je n'aime pas la chanson parce que la mélodie est **nul / nulle**.

2 J'adore la chanson parce que les paroles (f) sont **amusants / amusantes**.

3 J'aime la chanson parce que le chanteur est **intéressant / intéressants**.

4 Je déteste la chanson parce que le rythme est **ennuyeux / ennuyeuse**.

5 J'aime bien la chanson car la chanteuse est **bons / bonne**.

 2 Write out the jumbled sentences in the correct order.

1 la assez chanson est démodée   La chanson est assez démodée. ....

2 très chanteur intéressant est le   ....

3 les ennuyeuses un peu paroles sont   ....

4 vraiment mélodie est originale la   ....

5 assez la chanteuse amusante est   ....

After the verb *jouer* (to play), use *du* for masculine instruments and *de la* for feminine instruments.

*Je joue **du** clavier.*

*Elle joue **de la** trompette.*

3 Fill in the gaps in the sentences with either *du* or *de la*, then translate them into English.

1   Elle joue tous les jours .... batterie (f).

....

2   Je joue .... violon (m) dans un orchestre.

....

3   Tu joues .... piano (m) avec qui?

....

4   Il joue .... guitare (f) dans un groupe.

....

5   Elles jouent .... clavier (m) ensemble.

....

Use a direct object pronoun (him/her/it/them) to replace a noun. It goes **in front of** the verb. **G**

Masculine:	**le**	Je **le** trouve intéressant.	I find him/it interesting.
Feminine:	**la**	Je **la** trouve amusante.	I find her/it funny.
Plural:	**les**	Je **les** trouve démodé(e)s.	I find them old-fashioned.

The adjectives still need to agree!

---

4 Circle the correct direct object pronoun (*le, la* or *les*) in each sentence.

1   J'adore la chanson. Je **le / la / les** trouve originale.

2   Comment tu trouves le chanteur? Je **le / la / les** trouve très beau.

3   Je n'aime pas les paroles. Je **le / la / les** trouve ennuyeuses.

4   Comment tu trouves la mélodie? Je **le / la / les** trouve bête.

5   Je déteste les musiciens. Je **le / la / les** trouve assez démodés.

5 Translate the conversation into French.

- Do you like the new Jenifer song?
- I find **it** a bit boring.
- I find it very original.
- She plays the piano but, in my opinion, it's old-fashioned.
- **How** do you find the lyrics?
- I find them really rubbish!
- I love **Jenifer's music**.

Use *comment*.

This refers to 'the song' – *la chanson*.

'the music of Jenifer'

- Tu aimes la nouvelle chanson de Jenifer?
- ....
- ....
- ....
- ....
- ....
- ....
- ....
- ....

1 Rewrite the sentences to include the expression of frequency given in brackets.

> Expressions of frequency tend to go after the verb in French, e.g: *je joue* **souvent** *du clavier*; *il chante* **chaque semaine** *dans la chorale.*

1 J'écoute du hip-hop. (souvent)

....

2 J'écoute de la techno. (de temps en temps)

....

3 J'écoute du rock. (parfois)

....

4 J'écoute de la musique classique. (tout le temps)

....

2 Translate the sentences from exercise 1 into English.

> Make it sound natural in English. Don't just translate word for word. **T**

1 ....

2 ....

3 ....

4 ....

> Use **the comparative** to compare two or more things. **G**
>
> *plus* + adjective + *que*   more + adjective + **than**
>
> The adjective must agree with the **first noun** mentioned.
>
> *Le jazz est* **plus** *intéressant* **que** *le rock.*   Jazz is **more** interesting **than** rock.
> *La techno est* **plus** *originale* **que** *le rap.*   Techno is **more** original **than** rap.
>
> *meilleur/meilleure que* means 'better than'.

3 Circle the correct spelling of the adjective in each of these statements.

1	Le rap est plus	original	originale	que la techno.
2	La danse est plus	amusant	amusante	que le golf.
3	La musique classique est	meilleur	meilleure	que le rock.
4	Le théâtre est plus	intéressant	intéressante	que la géographie.
5	La cuisine est plus	grand	grande	que la salle de bains.
6	Le reggae est	meilleur	meilleure	que le jazz.

4 Write out the jumbled sentences in the correct order to form sentences using the comparative.

Use the spelling of the adjective (masculine/feminine) to work out which style of music needs to be at the start of each sentence.

1 le   reggae   plus   classique   est   que   la   musique   amusant

....

2 traditionnelle   la   est   plus   que   musique   R'n'B   relaxante   le

....

3 techno   la   est   le   plus   que   intéressante   jazz

....

4 le   que   est   meilleur   hip-hop   le   rap

....

G

The following negative expressions go **around the verb.**

ne … pas	(not)	→	Je n'écoute **pas** de jazz.	(I don't listen to jazz.)
ne … jamais	(never)	→	Je n'écoute **jamais** de jazz.	(I never listen to jazz.)

Remember that after a negative *du, de la* and *des* change to *de*.

5 Translate the sentences into French. Use all the advice on this double page to help.

1 I often listen to music.

....

2 I don't listen to rap because it's boring.

....

3 I never listen to classical music.

....

4 Hip-hop is more interesting than rock.

....

5 Jazz is better than reggae.

....

In sentences 4 and 5, don't forget the definite article (*le/la*) before each type of music.

Use the **imperfect tense** to say you **used to** do something. It can also mean **was doing** or **were doing** something.

To form the imperfect tense, take *-ons* off the *nous* form of the verb in the present tense, then add the endings. E.g. *nous jouons* ⟶ *jou-*

*je jou**ais***	I used to play / I was playing
*tu jou**ais***	you (singular) used to play / you were playing
*il/elle/on jou**ait***	he/she/we used to play / he/she was (we were) playing

Use the *nous* form 'stem', not the infinitive, as they are different in some verbs.

finir (to finish)	⟶	*nous finissons*	⟶	*finiss-*	⟶	*je finissais*
boire (to drink)	⟶	*nous buvons*	⟶	*buv-*	⟶	*je buvais*
faire (to do)	⟶	*nous faisons*	⟶	*fais-*	⟶	*je faisais*

The only verb with an irregular imperfect tense stem is *être*:

j'étais	I used to be / was
tu étais	you (singular) used to be / were
il/elle/on était	he/she/we used to be / he/she was (we were)

 1 **Draw lines to match up the French and English.**

1	j'aimais	a	I used to go
2	j'allais	b	I used to hate
3	j'avais	c	I used to like
4	je détestais	d	I used to wear
5	j'étais	e	I used to play
6	je mangeais	f	I used to have
7	je jouais	g	I used to be
8	je portais	h	I used to eat

 2 **Write the correct verbs to complete the sentences and the crossword.**

Quand j'étais petit(e), …

1 je .... toujours un short.

2 je .... beaucoup sur l'ordinateur.

3 je .... les araignées.

4 j' .... à l'école primaire.

5 j' .... assez paresseux.

6 j' .... les cheveux longs.

7 j' .... les dessins animés.

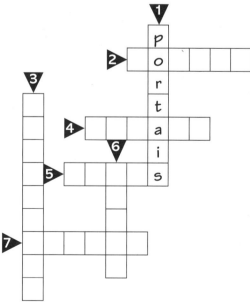

3 Add the correct ending to the verbs to form the imperfect tense, then translate into English.

1 je jou .....ais..........   ....I used to play...............

2 elle port ....

3 tu buv ....

4 il finiss ....

5 tu ét ....

6 elle habit ....

4 Rewrite the backwards words the right way round to form sentences in the imperfect tense.

1 dnauQ siaté'j titep, ej siadrager sel seriatnemucod ceva nom erèrf.
   Quand j'étais petit, ...
   ....

2 À egâ'l ed xid sna, elle tiatrop suot sel sruoj enu epuj.
   ....

3 aM erèitam eéréférp, tiaté'c sel shtam, siam tnanetniam, tse'c SPE'l.
   ....

4 À egâ'l ed qnic sna, li tiava sel xuevehc sdnolb.
   ....

5 Read the interview with Lady Orchardleigh and complete the French translation.

1	I used to live in a small	....
	apartment in town	.... en ville
2	but now, I live	mais maintenant, ...
3	in a big house	dans ....
	in the country.	à la campagne.
4	My daughter used to hate cars,	Ma fille ....,
5	but she used to love cinema.	.... le cinéma.
6	She always used to play with	.... toujours avec
	her friends,	....,
7	but now she plays	....
	with cows!	.... des vaches!

Use the **present tense** to talk about what you **do** or **are doing**.		Use the **near future tense** to talk about what you **are going to do**.	
je fais	I do / I am doing	*je vais faire*	I am going to do
je vais	I go / I am going	*je vais aller*	I am going to go
je chante	I sing / I am singing	*je vais chanter*	I am going to sing
j'écris	I write / I am writing	*je vais écrire*	I am going to write
j'habite	I live / I am living	*je vais habiter*	I am going to live

VERT 1 Which tense are the verbs in? Write P for 'present' or NF for 'near future'.

1 je fais — P
2 je danse —
3 je vais voyager —
4 je vais prendre —
5 je vais visiter —
6 je suis —
7 j'écris —
8 je vais faire —
9 je vais —

VERT 2 Complete the French translations of these sentences. Use the correct time expression from the box to start you off.

l'année prochaine   l'été prochain   la semaine prochaine   à l'avenir

1 Next year, I am going to travel to the USA.

......................................, ... aux États-Unis.

2 In the future, I am going to write a novel.

......................................, ... un roman.

3 Next week, I am going to sing in the choir.

......................................, ... dans la chorale.

4 Next summer, I am going to go to St Tropez.

......................................, ... à St Tropez.

VERT 3 Translate the sentences into French.

1 At the moment, I live in Paris, but next year, I am going to live in Marseille.
En *ce* moment, j'habite à Paris, mais ...

2 At the moment, I play tennis, but next summer, I am going to play golf.

3 At the moment, I write in an exercise book, but in the future, I am going to write on a computer.

un cahier exercise book

Dynamo 3 © Pearson Education Ltd 2020

> The imperfect tense means **used to** (look back to page 40 for full details).
> It can also be used for **descriptions** in the past.
>
> | | |
> |---|---|
> | *Mon chien **était** petit.* | My dog **was** small. |
> | *Mon copain **avait** les cheveux longs.* | My friend **had** long hair. |
> | ***Il y avait** deux salles de classe.* | **There were** two classrooms. |
> | ***C'était** assez ennuyeux.* | **It was** quite boring. |

G

1 **Choose the correct imperfect tense verb to complete each sentence.**

1   Mon école primaire .... Radyr Primary.

2   J'.. les maths, l'anglais et l'histoire-géo.

3   Le bâtiment .... très vieux.

4   J'.. les cheveux longs et blonds.

> étudiais   s'appelait
> avais   était

> Use the **comparative** to compare two or more things, no matter what tense you are using.
>
> **plus** + adjective (+ **que**)   **more** + adjective (**than**)
> **moins** + adjective (+ **que**)   **less** + adjective (**than**)
>
> The adjective must agree with the first noun mentioned.
>   *Ma tortue était **plus** intéressant**e** que mon hamster.*
>
> *Meilleur(e)(s)* means 'better'.
>
> Comparatives don't always have to include *que*.
>   *Le film était **plus** intéressant.*   The film was **more** interesting.

G

> Which tense – present or imperfect?

2 **Translate the comparative sentences into English.**

1   J'étais beaucoup moins sportif que ma sœur. ....

2   Le bâtiment était plus vieux que mon grand-père! ....

3   Mon emploi du temps est meilleur que l'an dernier. ....

4   Cette année, les devoirs sont moins difficiles. ....

3 **Underline all the English parts in this tangled text. Then rewrite the whole text in French on a separate sheet.**

> 'stricter' = 'more strict'

> I love mon collège, but I didn't use to like mon école primaire. It was assez
> ennuyeux et the teachers étaient beaucoup stricter qu'au collège. Ici, les profs
> sont better. Cependant, à l'école primaire, there were cent élèves en tout,
> ce qui was really sympa. Last year, ma matière préférée was les maths, but now,
> je trouve le français more fun.

Use the perfect tense to say what you **did** or **have done**. Remember the 1-2-3 rule:

1 subject pronoun   **2** helping verb *(avoir or être)*   **3** past participle

j'ai dansé	I danced
tu as dansé	you (singular) danced
il/elle/on a dansé	he/she/we danced
nous avons dansé	we danced
vous avez dansé	you (plural/polite) danced
ils/elles ont dansé	they danced

Some verbs have irregular past participles:

boire (to drink) – *bu*   *voir* (to see) – *vu*   *prendre* (to take) – *pris*

The verb *aller* uses *être* as the helping verb instead of *avoir*:

*je **suis** allé(e)*   I went

1 **Draw lines to fill the gaps in these perfect tense sentences.**

1 Je suis   acheté   à un concert à Wigan.

2 J'ai   pris   mon groupe préféré, DynamoStars.

3 J'ai   dansé   beaucoup de photos.

4 J'ai   allée   pendant deux heures.

5 J'ai   vu   un tee-shirt.

To make a perfect tense sentence negative, put *ne ... pas* around the part of the helping verb *(avoir* or *être)*. Remember that *ne* shortens to *n'* in front of a vowel.

j'ai mangé	I ate	*je **n'**ai **pas** mangé*	I didn't eat
j'ai bu	I drank	*je **n'**ai **pas** bu*	I didn't drink
je suis allé(e)	I went	*je **ne** suis **pas** allé(e)*	I didn't go

2 **Change the five sentences from exercise 1 into negative sentences.**

1 Je ne ....

2 Je n' ....

3 ....

4 ....

5 ....

Un, *une* and *des* all change to <u>*de*</u> when used after *ne ... pas*.

VERT 3 Separate out the word snakes to form perfect tense sentences.

> Watch out for negatives.
> You may need to add in an apostrophe.

1 jenesuispasalléenville ....

2 nousavonsbuducoca ....

3 jaiadoréleconcert ....

4 ellenapaschanté ....

5 tuasprisdesphotos ....

You can use **est-ce que** to form questions in the perfect tense.

G

Pourquoi **est-ce que** _tu es allé(e) au concert?_	<u>Why</u> did you go to the concert?
Quand **est-ce que** _tu es allé(e) au concert?_	<u>When</u> did you go to the concert?
Comment **est-ce que** _tu es allé(e) au concert?_	<u>How</u> did you go to the concert?
Qui **est-ce que** _tu as vu?_	<u>Who</u> did you see?
_Qu'_**est-ce que** _tu as acheté?_	<u>What</u> did you buy?

VERT 4 Fill in the missing words to translate the questions into French.

1 Why did you buy a tee-shirt? .... est-ce que .... un tee-shirt?

2 How did you go to Méribel? .... est-ce que .... à Méribel?

3 When did we dance? .... est-ce que ....?

4 What did we drink? .... est-ce que ....?

> Remember you will need the 1-2-3 of the perfect tense in the second gap each time.

VERT 5 Translate the sentences into French.

1 I didn't go to Paris last year.

....

2 I saw my favourite singer and **it was** great. [_c'était_]

....

3 What did you buy as a souvenir?

....

Autrefois … aujourd'hui …

• Using the present and imperfect tenses together

> Use the **imperfect tense** to say how things **were** or **used to be**. Use the **present tense** to say how things are **now**.
> Look at the verb tables on pages 78–80 for full verb paradigms in both tenses.
>
> | imperfect tense | | present tense | |
> |---|---|---|---|
> | je regard**ais** | nous regard**ions** | je regard**e** | nous regard**ons** |
> | tu regard**ais** | vous regard**iez** | tu regard**es** | vous regard**ez** |
> | il/elle/on regard**ait** | ils/elles regard**aient** | il/elle/on regard**e** | ils/elles regard**ent** |
>
> Remember *on* can be used to mean 'people' (in general).

1 Write the pairs of verb phrases into the correct cloud.

c'est	j'achetais
nous utilisions	tu écoutes
tu écoutais	on va
on allait	nous utilisons
j'achète	c'était

imperfect tense

j'achetais

present tense

j'achète

2 Circle the tense (imperfect or present) that each sentence needs, then fill in the gap(s) with the correct version of the verb(s) in brackets.

1 Il y a dix ans, je ……………… (jouer) toujours avec mon petit frère. **imperfect / present**

2 Aujourd'hui, le tennis ……………… (être) plus intéressant que le golf. **imperfect / present**

3 Quand j'……………… (être) jeune, j'……………… (avoir) les cheveux longs. **imperfect / present**

4 Aujourd'hui, j'……………… (écouter) de la musique en streaming. **imperfect / present**

3 Use the words below to translate the sentences into French.

1 It was a difficult day for me.

C'était …

………………………………………………………………………………………………

2 Forty years **ago**, people used to buy audio cassettes.

il y a

………………………………………………………………………………………………

3 In the past, radio was a lot more popular than now.

………………………………………………………………………………………………

Dynamo 3 © Pearson Education Ltd 2020

Remember there are two past tenses.

The **imperfect tense** talks about what you **used to do** or **were doing** in the past.

The **perfect tense** talks about what you **did** (usually single actions) in the past.

imperfect tense	
stem + ending	
je jouais	I was playing
tu allais	you were going
il faisait	he was doing/making

perfect tense	
avoir/être + past participle	
j'ai joué	I played
tu es allé(e)	you went
il a fait	he did/made

4 **Underline the subject and verb in each sentence and then tick the appropriate column to show which tense is used.**

> You need to underline **two verbs** and tick **two boxes** for questions 4 and 6.

	perfect	imperfect	present
1 J'ai écouté de la musique classique.	☐	☐	☐
2 Ma mère achète toujours des billets de concert.	☐	☐	☐
3 Ce matin, il faisait très beau temps.	☐	☐	☐
4 Nous jouions au tennis quand elle est tombée.	☐	☐	☐
5 D'habitude, vous préférez les films romantiques.	☐	☐	☐
6 Il courait en montagne et il a perdu une de ses baskets!	☐	☐	☐

5 **Translate sentences 4 and 6 from exercise 4 into English.**

4 ....

6 ....

6 **Translate Jérémy's story into English.**

> Hier matin, ma femme et moi, nous étions chez nous. Elle lisait le journal et elle écoutait de la musique classique, donc j'ai décidé de faire une promenade avec le chien. Malheureusement, j'ai perdu le chien et je suis rentré à la maison tout seul. Ma femme était furieuse! Mais trente minutes plus tard, un voisin a trouvé le chien. Quelle chance!

une femme	*woman / wife*
donc	*so, therefore*
malheureusement	*unfortunately*
quelle chance!	*how lucky!*

....

....

....

....

....

> Use the **present tense** to refer to what you do **now**, or what something is like **now** (see page 6). **G**
>
> *Je regarde la télé.*   *J'adore le hip-hop.*   *La chanson est originale.*
>
> Use the **perfect tense** to refer to what you **did** or what **happened** in the **past** (see page 44).
>
> *J'ai mangé une pizza.*   *Je suis allé(e) à un concert.*   *J'ai bu du coca.*

1 Present tense or perfect tense? Copy each verb into the correct box.

je joue	j'ai dansé
elle chante	elle a joué
j'ai mangé	j'adore
tu préfères	je suis allée
tu es allé	il a fait
il écoute	tu regardes

present tense

perfect tense

2 Complete the table with the given verbs in the present and perfect tenses, in both French and English.

	subject	infinitive	present tense	perfect tense
1	je	chanter	je chante – I sing	j'ai chanté – I sang
2	tu	danser		
3	je	jouer		
4	tu	adorer		
5	tu	écouter		
6	je	aller		

3 Translate the sentences into French.

1 I **play the** guitar and I sing as well.

> Use *jouer + du / de la.*

....

2 Last week, I went to **a Stormzy concert**.

> Word order will be 'a concert of Stormzy'.

....

3 I love hip-hop but I prefer rap.

....

4 **On** Sunday, I went to Paris.

> No need for a word for 'on' in French.

....

5 Last night, I ate in a restaurant.

....

> You can form questions in any tense using this structure:
>   question word + *est-ce que* + subject + verb + rest of sentence
> For yes/no questions, just leave out the question word and start the question with *Est-ce que …?*
> | | |
> |---|---|
> | **perfect tense:** | *Pourquoi <u>est-ce que</u> tu es allé(e) en Angleterre?* |
> | **imperfect tense:** | *Où <u>est-ce qu'il</u> jouait au tennis?* |
> | **present tense:** | *<u>Est-ce que</u> vous préférez la musique classique ou le rap?* |
> | ***vouloir* + infinitive:** | *Quand <u>est-ce que</u> tu veux aller au cinéma avec moi?* |

1 **ROUGE** Unjumble the French questions to translate the English questions.

1   Why do you want to become a musician?

devenir   est-ce   que   tu   musicien   pourquoi   veux

....

2   When were they watching the film?   qu'ils   est-ce   le   film   quand   regardaient

....

3   Where was she born?   qu'elle   où   est   née   est-ce

....

4   Do you prefer maths or science?

les   préférez   que   vous   maths   les   est-ce   sciences   ou

....

2 **ROUGE** Draw lines to match up the two halves of each question, then choose two questions to translate into English.

1   Est-ce qu'elle   a   as fait tes devoirs?

2   Quand est-ce que tu   b   jouez au golf d'habitude?

3   Pourquoi est-ce que nous c   veut aller au centre commercial?

4   Où est-ce que vous   d   apprenions le portugais?

....

....

3 **ROUGE** Write a question for each answer below. Keep the same tense, but use the *tu* form of the verb.

1   • ....

  ▪ J'ai quitté la Croatie en 1999.

2   • ....

  ▪ Non, je n'aime pas trop habiter à Paris.

3   • ....

  ▪ Je gagne huit cents euros par mois.

- When translating, read the whole sentence or paragraph before you look at individual words.
- Work out unknown words using the words you do know, the context, and a bit of common sense!

T

VERT 1 Complete the missing words in the translations.

1 Je n'aime pas la chanson car la mélodie est nulle.

I .... rubbish

2 À mon avis, le jazz est plus intéressant que la techno.

In ...., ... techno.

3 L'année prochaine, je vais visiter le château.

Next ...., ... castle.

4 Le weekend dernier, elle a acheté un poster.

Last ...., ... poster.

VERT ROUGE 2 Read the email and translate the underlined sections into English.

Mon copain Éric chante dans un groupe **1** au collège. Quand **2** il était petit,
3 il jouait de la batterie, mais **4** maintenant, **5** il préfère chanter. Le groupe s'appelle
QMS et le mois dernier, **6** ils ont gagné un prix dans un concours de talent.
7 C'était super! En avril, ils vont faire un concert **8** dans un vieux cinéma près du collège.

1 ....
2 ....
3 ....
4 ....

5 ....
6 ....
7 ....
8 ....

3 ROUGE Underline all the French parts in this tangled text. Then rewrite the whole text in English.

Quand j'étais petit, I used to wear une
casquette rouge tous les jours – c'était
awful! À l'école primaire, je n'aimais pas the
teachers, mais au collège, they are meilleurs,
heureusement. En ce moment, I find les
maths plus easy que le français. Le weekend
dernier, je faisais my French homework
quand a cat est entré dans ma bedroom.

....
....
....
....
....
....
....
....
....

1 Choose and shade a box from each column to translate each sentence into French. Use a different colour for each sentence.

1 She plays guitar in a group.

2 Techno is more original than rap.

3 I am going to travel by car.

4 I didn't go to the concert.

je vais	est plus	dans	que le rap
elle joue	voyager	originale	au concert
la techno	de la guitare	pas allé	voiture
je ne	suis	en	un groupe

- Sometimes there will need to be more words in French than English, and sometimes fewer!
- Check any time expressions, as well as the verb itself, to work out which tense you need.

T

2 Count the number of words in the English sentence. Predict whether it will be more or fewer words in French, and then translate it into French to check if you were right!

	English	Prediction	La musique classique est ...	French
1 Classical music is better than jazz.	6	↑	....	8
2 Tomorrow, I am going to play tennis.	☐	☐	....	☐
3 Last weekend, she watched a film.	☐	☐	....	☐
4 In the past, people used to buy CDs.	☐	☐	....	☐

fort(e)	loud
on	people

3 Translate the sentences into French.

1 When I was little, I used to like pop music, but now I prefer classical music.

....

2 Last weekend, she went to a concert and the music was very loud.

....

3 In primary school, the teachers were better.

....

4 In the past, people used to buy cassettes.

....

Point de départ

- **Describing a photo**

Use the articles *du*, *de la*, *de l'* or *des* to say 'some'. They are useful for talking about food and drink: *Je voudrais du pain*. I would like **some** bread.

du *pain* (m)	**some** bread
de la *viande* (f)	**some** meat
de l'*eau* (vowel)	**some** water
des *haricots* (pl)	**some** beans

'Some' is optional in English: She is eating some bread. / She is eating bread.

1 Choose the correct article (*du*, *de la*, *de l'*, *des*) to fill each gap.

Sur la photo, il y a .... pain (m), ... riz (m) avec .... légumes (pl), une pomme (f) et .... salade (f).

Why does it say **une pomme** and not **de la pomme**?

The present tense in French has two possible meanings in English:

je mange	I eat <u>or</u> I am eating
elles portent	they wear <u>or</u> they are wearing

2 Complete the English translations of these sentences.

1 Je mange des biscuits et une banane.

I am eating ....

2 Elle boit du thé avec du lait.

She is drinking ....

3 Les enfants jouent dans le parc.

The children are ....

4 Il porte un tee-shirt bleu et jaune.

He ....

5 Elles ramassent des bouteilles en plastique.

They ....

6 Tu fais tes devoirs aujourd'hui?

.... homework today?

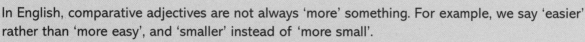

G

The comparative is used to compare two things:

plus … que / moins … que   more … than / less … than

In English, comparative adjectives are not always 'more' something. For example, we say 'easier' rather than 'more easy', and 'smaller' instead of 'more small'.
Remember that the adjective needs to agree with the **first noun** mentioned.

3 Choose and shade a box from each column to translate the sentences into French. Use a different colour for each sentence. Then write them out in full underneath.

à mon avis	le repas	des boîtes	plus savoureux	à la	bonbons
les enfants	ramassent	sont moins	pizza	que le repas	en plastique
je pense que	les chips	français est	et des	que les	cantine
ils	mangent	de la	saines	bouteilles	britannique

1   In my opinion, crisps are less healthy than sweets.

   ....

2   They are collecting cans and plastic bottles.

   ....

3   I think that the French meal is tastier than the British meal.

   ....

   ....

4   The children are eating pizza in the canteen.

   ....

4 Translate the sentences into French to describe the photo.

1   In the photo, there are two boys and two girls.

   ....

2   They are watching a tennis match.

   ....

3   The two boys are wearing tee-shirts.

   ....

| **à droite** | *on the right* |
| **en jean** | *denim* |

4   The girl on the right is wearing a denim jacket.

   ....

When translating phrases such as 'they are watching', don't be tempted to use part of the verb 'to be' (*être*). Remember that in French 'they are watching' is the same as 'they watch'.

Est-ce que tu manges de la viande?

• Present tense, negatives, accuracy in translation

G

Negatives form a 'sandwich' around the verb:

| ne … pas | not | Je **ne** mange **pas** de viande. |
| ne … jamais | never | Je **ne** mange **jamais** de viande. |

Ne shortens to *n'* before a vowel.

Remember that the articles *un, une, du, de la, de l'* and *des* all change to **de** after a negative.

VERT 1 Underline the <u>verb</u> and circle the two parts of the negative in each sentence.

1   Je ne mange pas de viande.

2   Elle ne mange jamais de poisson.

3   Je ne bois pas de lait.

4   Il n'aime pas le végétarisme.

5   Elles ne boivent jamais de café.

6   Nous ne sommes pas végétariens.

> *le végétarisme*   vegetarianism

VERT 2 Translate the first three sentences from exercise 1 into English.

1   ....

2   ....

3   ....

VERT ROUGE 3 Draw lines to match up the French and English expressions.

1	je suis pour	a	I am against
2	je suis contre	b	I don't agree
3	à mon avis	c	I think that
4	je pense que	d	I am for
5	tu es d'accord?	e	I agree
6	je suis d'accord	f	in my opinion
7	je ne suis pas d'accord	g	do you agree?

VERT ROUGE 4 Fill in the missing words in the parallel sentences.

I don't like ....

Do you agree?

....

I never eat meat.

.... le végétarisme.

....?

Non, je ne suis pas d'accord.

....

....

There are several other negative expressions that also form a 'sandwich' around the verb:

ne … plus	no longer / not any more
ne … rien	nothing / not anything

G

5 Write accurate sentences in French, using the words and pictures to build your sentences. All sentences will start with *il*, *elle*, *ils* or *elles*. Then translate your sentences into English.

1   ne … pas   *Il ne mange pas de viande.*
....

2 ne … plus ....
....

3  ne … jamais   ....
....

4  ne … rien   ....
....

5   ne … plus   ....
....

Take care with cognates. Have you got the correct spelling? Are there any accents?

T

6 Translate this paragraph into French.

In my opinion, vegetarianism is very important because we must respect animals and the planet. I no longer eat meat and I never use animal products. Do you agree?

....
....
....
....

1 Choose the correct present tense verb from the box for each sentence.

> est
> habite
> boit
> mange

1 Le tigre .... à la campagne.

2 Il .... de la viande et il .... de l'eau.

3 Le tigre .... menacé par la chasse.

G

Some words or phrases are followed by an infinitive:

il faut + infinitive   you must

il ne faut pas + infinitive   you must not

> **Il faut** *planter des arbres.*   **You must** plant trees.
> **Il ne faut pas** *voyager en voiture.*   **You must not** travel by car.

pour + infinitive   in order to

> **pour** *aider les animaux*   **in order to** help the animals

---

 T

 2 Translate the sentences into English.

1 Pour aider la planète, il ne faut pas voyager en avion.

In order to help the planet, ...

Don't just reach for a dictionary! Look at any clues in the sentence and make an educated guess about what you think the meaning might be.

....

....

2 Pour réduire les déchets, il ne faut pas acheter de bouteilles en plastique.

....

....

3 Pour protéger les animaux, il faut arrêter la déforestation.

....

....

Do you need the verb in its infinitive form, or does it need to change to match the subject of the verb?

 3 Circle the correct option for each verb.

1 Le panda géant **habiter** / **habite** dans la forêt.

2 Pour **aider** / **aide** le panda géant, il faut **protéger** / **protège** la forêt.

3 Le panda géant **être** / **est** menacé par la pollution.

4 Pour **conserver** / **conserve** son habitat, il ne faut pas **polluer** / **pollue** les rivières.

The superlative is used to say 'the **most dangerous** animal', 'the **smallest** species', etc. Adjectives that come **before** the noun work like this:

le plus petit dinosaure	**the smallest** dinosaur
la plus grande grenouille	**the biggest** frog

Adjectives that come **after** the noun work like this:

le mammifère *le plus dangereux*	**the most dangerous** mammal
la baleine *la plus lente*	**the slowest** whale

4 **Look at these nouns and adjectives, then write superlative sentences using them as a starting point.**

ROUGE

1   la pizza   populaire   l'hawaïenne

 .....La pizza la plus populaire, c'est l'hawaïenne.............................

2   le mammifère marin   grand   la baleine bleue

....

3   la matière   utile   le français

   ....

4   l'oiseau volant   grand   l'albatros hurleur    | *volant*   *flying* |

....

5 **Underline the English words, then rewrite the tangled text completely in French.**

ROUGE

> The fastest animal du monde, c'est le guépard. It is a large
> mammifère carnassier qui lives in Africa et en Asie de l'Ouest.
> The cheetah est classé comme vulnérable.
> In order to conserve l'habitat des guépards, you must not
> polluer les lacs and rivers.

....

....

....

....

....

Use the **present tense** to say what you do **now**, and the **perfect tense** to say what you **have done**.

present tense			perfect tense	
j'organise	I organise		j'ai organisé	I organised
je recycle	I recycle		j'ai recyclé	I recycled
j'achète	I buy		j'ai acheté	I bought
je vais	I go		je suis allé(e)	I went

1 Can you remember these past tense time phrases? Draw lines to match them up.

1 vendredi dernier

2 hier

3 l'année dernière

4 la semaine dernière

a last week

b last year

c yesterday

d last Friday

2 Separate out the word snakes and write the sentences in full. Is the sentence in the present tense or perfect tense?

present   perfect

1 j'habitedansunvillageenangleterre

.... ☐ ☐

2 récemmentj'airecyclédupapier

.... ☐ ☐

3 leweekenddernierjesuisalléeenville

.... ☐ ☐

4 touslesjoursjevaisaucollègeàpied

.... ☐ ☐

5 lundidernierj'airamassédesdéchets

.... ☐ ☐

3 Write out the jumbled perfect tense sentences in the correct order. Each one begins with a time phrase.

1 dernière   anti-plastique   la   campagne   j'ai   organisé   semaine   une

....

2 acheté   des   à   la   scolaire   produits   bio   hier   cantine   j'ai

....

3 à   dernier   je   amis   suis   vendredi   collège   allé   pied   avec   au   mes

....

Use the **present tense** to talk about what you do **now**.
Use the **perfect tense** to talk about what you **did** or **have done**.
Use the **imperfect tense** to talk about what you **used to do** or **were doing**.

present tense	perfect tense	imperfect tense
je retrouve	j'ai retrouvé	je retrouvais
tu recycles	tu as recyclé	tu recyclais
il/elle/on va	il/elle/on est allé(e)(s)	il/elle/on allait
nous organisons	nous avons organisé	nous organisions
vous achetez	vous avez acheté	vous achetiez
ils/elles rentrent	ils/elles sont rentré(e)s	ils/elles rentraient

1 Circle the correct option for each verb.

> Look for clues in the sentence to identify the tense needed.

1 À l'école primaire, **je joue** / **je jouais** au foot à la récré.

2 Hier, **il va** / **il est allé** au supermarché en voiture.

3 Maintenant, **j'ai utilisé** / **j'utilise** une bouteille réutilisable.

4 Quand elle était jeune, **elle recyclait** / **elle recycle** le plastique.

2 Decide which tense you need, then translate each phrase into French.

1 they (m) went _ils sont allés_

2 we (on) used to live ....

3 she travels ....

4 I refused ....

5 they (f) recycle ....

6 he was buying ....

3 Rewrite the backwards words and translate into English.

1 dnauq j'siaté titep, ej en siasiaf neir ruop redia al etènalp

Quand j'étais petit, ...

When I was little, ...

2 xua snisagam, elle esufer sruojuot sed scas ne euqitsalp

....

....

3 el dnekeew reinred, sli tnos sélla ua ertnec ed egalcycer

....

....

Je voudrais changer le monde …

• Conditional tense, *vouloir* and *aimer*

 G

Je voudrais (from *vouloir*, 'to want') and *j'aimerais* (from *aimer*, 'to like') both mean 'I would like'. They are examples of the conditional tense:

je voudrais	I would like	*nous voudrions*	we would like
tu voudrais	you would like	*vous voudriez*	you would like
il/elle/on voudrait	he/she/we would like	*ils/elles voudraient*	they would like

Both *je voudrais* and *j'aimerais* can be followed by an infinitive to say what you **would like to do**:

Je voudrais manger *moins de viande.*   **I would like to eat** less meat.
Elle aimerait acheter *plus de produits bio.*   **She would like to buy** more organic products.

 1 Circle the correct option to complete each sentence.

1 Je voudrais **voyager** / **voyage** en France en train.

2 Je voudrais **achète** / **acheter** moins de vêtements.

3 Je voudrais **fais** / **faire** du travail bénévole.

4 Je ne voudrais pas **utiliser** / **utilise** moins de plastique.

5 Je ne voudrais pas **mange** / **manger** moins de viande.

 2 Choose the correct word from the box to complete each sentence.

> voudrais
> recycler
> plastique
> aider
> changement
> être
> voudrais

1 Est-ce que tu voudrais .... les animaux menacés?

2 Je voudrais combattre le .... climatique.

3 Tu .... organiser une campagne anti-déchets.

4 Je ne .... pas .... membre d'un groupe écolo.

5 Je voudrais .... des sacs en ....

 3 Write out the words in the correct order to make negative conditional tense sentences.

> *Ne … pas* goes around the **first** verb – *je ne voudrais pas faire* (I would **not** like to do).

1 | je | aimerais | en | plastique | pas | n' | utiliser | de | bouteilles |

Je n'aimerais pas ....

2 | avion | ne | elle | pas | voyager | voudrait | en |

....

3 | tu | pas | faire | ne | travail | de | bénévole | voudrais |

....

4 | aimerait | il | acheter | pas | vêtements | plus | n' | de |

....

4 Complete the sentences with the correct part of *voudr–*. Then fill in the crossword.

1 Ils .... organiser une campagne anti-déchets.

2 Nous .... utiliser moins de plastique.

3 Je ne .... pas acheter plus de produits bio.

4 Tu .... utiliser le train et le bus.

5 Vous ne .... jamais manger de viande.

6 Elle .... faire du travail bénévole.

5 Translate the sentences from exercise 4 into English.

1 They would like ...

2 ....

3 ....

4 ....

5 ....

6 ....

6 Underline all the French words, then rewrite the tangled text completely in English.

Mon copain Raj fait lots of things pour aider l'environnement. Last year at school, il a organisé une campagne anti-déchets, which was très **efficace**. En plus, il ramasse toujours des boîtes and plastic bottles et il va au centre de recyclage every weekend. À l'avenir, il aimerait to use more produits bio et acheter fewer vêtements.

My friend Raj ...

....

....

....

....

....

....

....

Look for any clues as to what tense is needed – present, perfect, or conditional.

The adjective '*efficace*' describes the campaign. What could it mean?

JE DIS NON AUX DÉCHETS

> • Look out for any key phrases that can't be translated word for word, e.g. *il faut* ('you must').
> • Pay attention to verbs and time expressions to help you identify the tense of the sentence (past/present/future/conditional).

T

1 Choose and shade a box from each column to translate the sentences into English. Use a different colour for each sentence.

you	would like	eats	to school	plastic
she	I	went	paper	and bottles
I	never	recycle	less	or fish
yesterday	must	to use	meat	on foot

1 Elle ne mange jamais de viande ou de poisson.

2 Je voudrais utiliser moins de plastique.

3 Il faut recycler le papier et les bouteilles

4 Hier, je suis allé au collège à pied.

2 Complete the English translations.

1 Il ne faut pas utiliser plus d'énergie.   .... more energy

2 Dans le repas, il y a du riz et du fromage.   In the meal, ...

3 Elle mange une glace à la plage.   She ....

4 À mon avis, la viande est très savoureuse.   ...., meat is ....

5 Hier, j'ai ramassé des déchets.   Yesterday, ...

6 Il voudrait faire du travail bénévole.   .... voluntary work

3 Underline the six errors in the English translation of this text, then draw a line from each error to one of the boxes. Write the correct English words in the boxes.

> Je suis pour le véganisme car la production de viande est mauvaise pour l'environnement. Je pense qu'il faut manger plus de fruits et de légumes. Le weekend dernier, j'ai mangé dans un fast-food avec mes parents – ils ont pris des hamburgers, mais moi, j'ai choisi le nouveau sandwich végétarien. C'était délicieux.

[................]   [................]   [................]

> I am against veganism because the production of meat is good for the environment. I think that people should eat more fruit and vegetables. Next weekend, I am going to eat at a fast-food restaurant with my parents – we had hamburgers, but me, I chose the new vegetarian sandwich. It is delicious.

[................]   [................]   [................]

- You need to look at the meaning of the whole sentence – for example, *il faut* + **infinitive** could be 'you must', 'we must' or 'people should' in English (among other things!).
- Also, *on* can be used to mean 'we', 'you', 'they' or 'people in general'.

VERT 1 Draw lines between the three sections to match up the English sentence and the two halves of the French sentence.

1	I never eat meat.	Hier, je suis allé	trop d'énergie.
2	You must not use too much energy.	Je ne mange jamais	au collège à pied.
3	Yesterday, I walked to school.	Il ne faut pas utiliser	moins de vêtements.
4	I would like to buy fewer clothes.	Je voudrais acheter	de viande.

VERT ROUGE 2 Read the passage and then number the French phrases (1–12) on the right to put the translation in the correct order.

In order to protect the planet, we need to do lots of things. I try to eat less meat and to go to school on foot or by bike.
At the supermarket, my dad doesn't buy animal products.
Last week, my friends and I collected rubbish in our village.

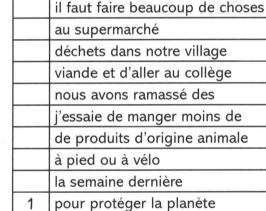

	mon père n'achète pas
	mes amis et moi
	il faut faire beaucoup de choses
	au supermarché
	déchets dans notre village
	viande et d'aller au collège
	nous avons ramassé des
	j'essaie de manger moins de
	de produits d'origine animale
	à pied ou à vélo
	la semaine dernière
1	pour protéger la planète

3 ROUGE Translate the sentences into French.

1 He would like to do voluntary work one day.

....

2 We organised an anti-plastic campaign.

....

3 I never drink milk or coffee.

....

4 At home, you must use less energy.

....

1 Choose a, b or c for each question.

1 A francophone country is a country where …
  a people still listen to French music on record players. ☐
  b the system language on your smartphone must be French. ☐
  c French is the most widely spoken language. ☐

2 The capital cities of France, Belgium and Switzerland are …
  a Paris, Bruges and Geneva. ☐
  b Paris, Brussels and Bern. ☐
  c Paris, Antwerp and Zurich. ☐

3 Three cities in the French-speaking parts of Canada are …
  a Montreal, Trois-Rivières and Quebec. ☐
  b Quebec, Vancouver and Toronto. ☐
  c Trois-Rivières, Montreal and Vancouver. ☐

2 Find eight French-speaking countries in the wordsearch and write them out in the list on the right. Remember to include the article!

L	A	F	R	A	N	C	E	M	É	C	L	L
E	D	O	S	Ï	X	M	U	S	L	E	E	E
C	L	A	S	U	I	S	S	E	S	A	L	S
A	N	O	C	B	A	L	C	É	A	B	U	L
N	L	E	S	É	N	É	G	A	L	X	X	A
A	C	X	U	A	R	É	M	G	S	E	E	T
D	L	D	B	E	G	G	I	M	U	E	M	U
A	L	A	T	A	B	S	F	L	G	A	B	N
A	S	Ï	L	D	É	C	D	Ï	A	G	O	I
L	A	B	E	L	G	I	Q	U	E	C	U	S
H	D	G	M	B	X	S	O	M	A	É	R	I
D	É	A	N	D	O	Ï	F	É	M	C	G	E
L	E	S	S	E	Y	C	H	E	L	L	E	S

la France
....
....
....
....
....
....
....

G

The **definite** article – **le** (m), **la** (f), **l'** (vowel), **les** (pl) – usually means 'the' in English.
The **indefinite** article – **un** (m), **une** (f), **des** (pl) – usually means 'a' or 'some' in English.
Sometimes the article is needed in French even when it is not needed in English:

*Je voudrais visiter **la** Suisse.*   I would like to visit Switzerland.
*Elle adore **la** soupe.*   She loves soup.

3 Circle the correct article in each sentence.

1 **Le / La** France est un beau pays.

2 C'est **un / une** château intéressant.

3 Il y a **un / des** magasins en ville.

4 Ils adorent **le / l'** chocolat.

5 Je n'aime pas **la / les** frites.

6 **La / L'** église est très vieille.

To say 'to the' or 'at the', follow this:

à + le = au
à + la = à la
à + l' = à l'
à + les = aux

Je vais **au** supermarché.

I go to the supermarket.

To say 'some', follow this:

de + le = du
de + la = de la
de + l' = de l'
de + les = des

Je voudrais **des** pommes.

I would like some apples.

G

4 Fill in the missing word(s) and then translate the sentences into English.

1 Je suis allée .... patinoire.   ....

2 Elle voudrait .... frites.   ....

3 Nous visiterons .... cathédrale.   ....

4 Tu as vu tous .... monuments?   ....

5 Je vais aller .... temples.   ....

6 Ils veulent .... melon.   ....

5 Underline the English words, then rewrite the tangled text completely in French.

Take care with <u>nouns</u> that need an article in French but not in English.

T

Next weekend, je vais visiter Belgium with ma famille. Samedi, je voudrais visiter some interesting monuments, et puis on Sunday, je veux regarder un match de foot at the national stadium because c'est hyper-cool! In the evening, nous allons aller to the cinema pour voir a French film.

....

....

....

....

....

....

....

1 Choose a, b or c for each question.

1 Mont-Saint-Michel is …
 a a French national holiday in October. ☐
 b a tidal island on the Normandy coast. ☐
 c the largest monastery in the French-speaking world. ☐

2 The *Viaduc de Millau* is …
 a a bridge on the A75 motorway in the south of France. ☐
 b the French parliament building in Paris. ☐
 c a duke in the era of King Louis XIV. ☐

3 Saint-Tropez is …
 a a special raspberry cake eaten in the summer months. ☐
 b a tourist town on the Mediterranean coast. ☐
 c the French patron saint of croissants. ☐

2 Fill in the crossword with the adjectives given. You will probably want to write in pencil!

> Try starting with the longest word!

petit

beau

unique

historique

mystérieux

impressionnant

intéressant

fabuleux

célèbre

grand

vieux

G

Adjectives must **agree** with the noun they are describing in both **gender** (masculine or feminine) and **number** (singular or plural).

adjective ending	masculine	feminine	masc. plural	fem. plural
consonant	important	importante	importants	importantes
–e	magnifique	magnifique	magnifiques	magnifiques
–eux	ennuyeux	ennuyeuse	ennuyeux	ennuyeuses
–l	nul	nulle	nuls	nulles
special cases	beau	belle	beaux	belles
	vieux	vieille	vieux	vieilles

Most adjectives come **after** the noun they describe, but a few come **before**:

grand(e)(s), petit(e)(s), beau(x)/belle(s), vieux/vieille(s), nouveau(x)/nouvelle(s)

Dynamo 3 © Pearson Education Ltd 2020

3 Complete the sentences with the correct French translation of the adjectives given.

1 interesting   Le pont du Gard est assez ....

2 famous   À Monaco, les magasins sont très ....

3 impressive   La tour Eiffel est un monument ....

4 large   Le mont Blanc est une .... montagne.

5 old   Le château de Versailles est un très .... château.

6 beautiful   Les Alpes françaises sont vraiment ....

4 Read the French text. For each missing word, find a suitable English adjective from the word in the wave. Then translate it into French to fill the gap.

beautifulfamoushistoricimpressivelargemagnificentmodernoriginalsmallboringold

L'hôtel du Cap-Éden-Roc est un hôtel de luxe très

(1) c.............................. situé dans le sud de la France. Il y a

deux bâtiments principaux – le château (2) o.................................

et un autre bâtiment (3) m.............................. avec piscine et

accès à la plage.

La piscine est assez (4) p.............................. mais il y a un

restaurant (5) h.............................. et un bar

(6) i.............................. juste à côté. Les chambres sont très

(7) g.............................. mais aussi assez chères. Il y a des

vues (8) m.............................. depuis les chambres, et c'est

une région très (9) b..............................!

5 Translate the second paragraph of the text in exercise 4 into English.

The swimming pool is ...

....

....

....

....

....

....

....

3 Réserver des excursions

• Using verbs with the infinitive

Choose a, b or c for each question.

1 *Le syndicat d'initiative* is another name for …
  a *l'office de tourisme.* ☐
  b *la patinoire.* ☐
  c *l'école maternelle.* ☐

2 Saint-Jean-de-Luz is a town in the south-west of France, near the border with …
  a Italy. ☐
  b Spain. ☐
  c Switzerland. ☐

3 *Une colonie de vacances* is …
  a a holiday brochure. ☐
  b a summer camp for youngsters. ☐
  c a long bank holiday weekend in May. ☐

Use the information below to crack the code and reveal the French phrases about likes and dislikes. Write the English translations in the table.

a	b	c	d	e	f	g	h	i	j	k	l	m	n	o	p	q	r	s	t	u	v	w	x	y	z
26	25		23	22	21			18	17			14					9		6					2	1

	Crack the French code	English
1	17 22 23 22 7 22 8 7 22 j e d	I hate
2	17 22 5 22 6 3	
3	17' 26 23 12 9 22	
4	17' 26 18 14 22	
5	17 22 13 22 5 22 6 3 11 26 8	
6	17 22 13' 26 18 14 22 11 26 8	

> You'll need to add in some accents to make your French sentences accurate!

The **infinitive** is the form of the verb meaning '**to** do something'.
It often ends in *–er* (e.g. *manger* – to eat).
Infinitives are used after opinion verbs and you can often translate them into English using '–ing'.

*J'adore **visiter** des musées.*   I love **visiting** museums.
*Elle n'aime pas **manger** au resto.*   She doesn't like **eating** out.

Dynamo 3 © Pearson Education Ltd 2020

3 Write out the words in the correct order to make sentences and translate into English.

1   monuments   pas   visiter   n'aime   des   je   historiques

Fr: ....

Eng: ....

2   adore   la   elle   aller   piscine   avec   à   moi

Fr: ....

Eng: ....

3   tennis   au   prochain   je   pas   jouer   veux   samedi   ne

Fr: ....

Eng: ....

The infinitive is also used after modal verbs such as *pouvoir* (can, to be able to), *vouloir* (to want to) and *devoir* (must, to have to).

*Tu **peux** jouer au badminton.*	You **can** (are able to) play badminton.
*On **peut** visiter le château.*	You **can** (are able to) visit the castle.
*Je **veux** aller au cinéma.*	I **want to** go to the cinema.
*Nous **devons** nettoyer la cuisine.*	We **must** (have to) clean the kitchen.

G

4 Complete each sentence with a suitable infinitive.

1   Je ne veux pas .... à parler portugais.

2   Elle déteste .... à la plage en été.

3   Nous devons .... à sept heures.

4   Il n'aime pas .... des musées.

5   On peut .... une visite guidée.

6   Tu adores .... au McDo!

5 Translate into French.

pendant   during
un éléphant   elephant

1   You can visit the water park during the holidays.

....

2   At the national park, we have to see the elephants.

....

3   I have to take my passport.

....

4   She doesn't like **sunbathing** on the beach.

....

....

'To sunbathe' is *se bronzer* – it's a reflexive verb in French, so make sure you include the correct reflexive pronoun.

1 Choose a, b or c for each question.

1 *Le Meilleur Pâtissier* is the French version of …
   a Love Island. ☐
   b Britain's Got Talent. ☐
   c The Great British Bake Off. ☐

2 Kylian Mbappé is a famous French …
   a footballer ☐
   b singer. ☐
   c politician. ☐

3 The correct French translation for 'Paralympic Games' is …
   a *les Games Paralympic.* ☐
   b *les Paralympiques Jeux.* ☐
   c *les Jeux Paralympiques.* ☐

The **present tense** is used to say what you **do** in general, or what you **are doing** at a particular time: *je porte* (I wear / I am wearing), *elle fait* (she does / she is doing).

Remember that although regular –er, –ir and –re verbs follow a pattern, there are also lots of important irregular verbs that don't follow any pattern (e.g. *avoir, être, faire*). If in doubt, check the verb tables on pages 78–80.

2 Translate the English phrases to complete the table. Then find the French verbs in the wordsearch.

J	E	P	O	R	T	E	E	M	I	C	J
E	E	O	S	A	P	I	A	N'	E	J	E
N	A	N	U	I	I	S	E	X	E	A	N'
E	E	O	E	B	A	L	C	N	I	B	H
P	T	G	É	S	J'	S	E	L	N	X	A
O	I	X	U	A	U	F	M	G	E	E	B
R	B	U	Q	I	A	I	E	J	A	L	I
T	A	A	T	I	B	S	S	L	G	A	T
E	H	J'	S	D	J'	C	D	P	A	G	E
P	J'	P	F	N	G	A	O	F	A	C	P
A	A	G	M	B	X	S	O	M	A	S	A
S	I	U	S	E	J	J	E	F	A	I	S

	English	French
1	I wear	*je porte*
2	I don't wear	
3	I have	
4	I don't have	
5	I am	
6	I am not	
7	I do	
8	I don't do	
9	I live	
10	I don't live	

Remember that the negative *ne … pas* makes a sandwich around the verb.

3 Draw lines to translate the sentences into French.

1	I am wearing grey trousers.	Il	sommes	un pantalon gris.
2	Are you working this weekend?	Nous	font	dans une grande ville.
3	He has long brown hair.	Ils	habitez	les cheveux longs et bruns.
4	We are very tired.	Tu	porte	très fatigués.
5	You live in a city.	Vous	a	ce weekend?
6	They are doing the washing-up.	Je	travailles	la vaisselle.

4 Underline the verbs in the English text and then tick the correct **eight** French verbs that you would need to translate the text. They aren't always direct translations.

Hello. My name is Zineb and I'm 14 years old. I live with my mum and my brother, who is quite annoying!
He wears really strange clothes and he just plays on the computer all day. At the moment, I'm preparing for my exams and listening to music on streaming.

ai	☐	habite	☐
aime	☐	habitons	☐
appelle	✓	joue	☐
as	☐	joué	☐
écoute	☐	porte	☐
écoutes	☐	portes	☐
es	☐	préfère	☐
est	☐	prépare	☐

5 Complete the missing parts of the parallel text about Enzo (@enzotaistoi).

1	.... une vedette française	Enzo is a French star
2	de la plateforme TikTok	....
3	.... actuellement très	and he is currently very well
4	connu dans le monde francophone.	known in ....
5	.... sa famille et	He lives with his family and
6	son chat (qui s'appelle Oreo)	.... (who is called Oreo)
7	.... de la France,	in the north of France,
8	près de la frontière belge.	....
9	Sur TikTok, ...	On TikTok, he has more than
10	deux millions d'abonnés.	....

On va jouer au foot!

• Near future tense (V/R) and simple future tense (R)

1 Choose a, b or c for each question.

1 The Cameroon national women's football team is known as …

  a *les Tortues.* ☐

  b *les Tigres.* ☐

  c *les Lionnes.* ☐

2 Brady Leman won the ski cross gold medal at the 2018 winter Olympics for …

  a France. ☐

  b Switzerland. ☐

  c Canada. ☐

3 One of the two continents never to have hosted the Olympics is …

  a Australasia. ☐

  b South America. ☐

  c Africa. ☐

G

The **near future tense** is used to talk about what someone is **going to do** in the future. It is formed using the verb *aller* + an infinitive.

je **vais** jouer	nous **allons** jouer
tu **vas** jouer	vous **allez** jouer
il/elle/on **va** jouer	ils/elles **vont** jouer

ne … pas forms a sandwich around the part of *aller* to make the verb negative.

  je **ne** vais **pas** jouer   I am **not** going to play

---

2 Translate the following near future tense phrases into French and then write them in the crossword.

1 we are going to play

  nous allons jouer
  ....

2 you (plural) are going to sleep

  ....

3 you (singular) are going to watch

  ....

4 they (f) are going to read

  ....

5 he is going to do

  ....

6 I am going to eat

  ....

Dynamo 3 © Pearson Education Ltd 2020

3 The words in these wordsnakes are not just wavy, but also in the wrong order! Write out the words in the correct order to make sentences.

1 *tennisjevaisnepasjouerau*

....

2 *vabeaucoupellemangerdepizza*

....

3 *vontnepasplageallerilsàla*

....

....

The **simple future tense** is used to talk about what **will** happen.
With regular **–er** verbs, you add these endings to the infinitive:

*je jouer**ai***	I will play	*nous jouer**ons***	we will play
*tu jouer**as***	you will play	*vous jouer**ez***	you will play
*il/elle/on jouer**a***	he/she/we will play	*ils/elles jouer**ont***	they will play

There are some important verbs which have irregular stems in the future tense:

avoir	→	*aur–*	→	*j'aur**ai***	→	I will have
être	→	*ser–*	→	*je ser**ai***	→	I will be
aller	→	*ir–*	→	*j'ir**ai***	→	I will go
faire	→	*fer–*	→	*je fer**ai***	→	I will do

G

---

4 Translate the sentences into French using the correct future tense.

1 she is going to do

....

2 they (m) will play

....

3 we will not win

....

4 I am not going to sleep

....

5 you (plural) will go

....

6 she is going to be

....

5 Translate this text into English on a separate sheet.

En ce moment, ma sœur joue pour l'équipe
de foot au lycée. Mais à l'avenir, elle jouera
pour l'équipe nationale – 'The Lionesses'.
Elle continuera à progresser et elle
travaillera dur. Un jour, avec son équipe, elle
gagnera des compétitions internationales.
Je suis très fier d'elle!

dur	hard
fier	proud

1 Choose a, b or c for each question.

1 Tofua is …
a the name of a particular style of bike in Morocco. ☐
b a volcanic island in the Pacific Ocean. ☐
c the brand name of a French meat substitute. ☐

2 In how many countries is French an official language?
a 19 ☐
b 29 ☐
c 39 ☐

3 In square miles, the island of Madagascar is …
a much bigger than the UK and Ireland. ☐
b roughly the same size as the UK and Ireland. ☐
c much smaller than the UK and Ireland. ☐

G

The **perfect tense** is used to talk about what happened in the past.

Most verbs use *avoir* as the helping verb in the perfect tense:
voyager ⟶ j'ai voyagé

Some verbs have irregular past participles:
voir ⟶ j'ai vu

Some verbs use *être* as the helping verb instead of *avoir*:
aller ⟶ je suis allé(e)

Ne … pas forms a sandwich around the part of *avoir* or *être* to make these verbs negative:
je n'ai pas voyagé   I didn't travel   je ne suis pas resté(e)   I didn't stay

2 Use the information below to crack the code and reveal the French perfect tense verbs. Write the English translations in the table.

a	b	c	d	e	f	g	h	i	j	k	l	m	n	o	p	q	r	s	t	u	v	w	x	y	z
25		2						8	9	10							17	18					22	23	24

	Crack the French code	English
1	8' 25 7 4 25 7 18 j' a i	I did
2	8' 25 7 1 13 11 11 3 12 1 3	
3	8' 25 7 20 19	
4	8 3 17 19 7 17 25 10 10 3 3	
5	8' 25 7 8 13 19 3	
6	8' 25 7 14 16 7 17	

You will need to add an accent (*é*) for some of the past participles.

Dynamo 3 © Pearson Education Ltd 2020

3 Rewrite the backwards perfect tense verbs and draw lines to match them with the English.

1	édrager ia'j	j'ai regardé	I bought
2	élla sius ej	....	I went
3	sirp sap ia'n ej	....	I chose
4	étehca ia'j	....	I danced
5	tiaf ia'j	....	I did
6	isiohc ia'j	....	I didn't play
7	uv sap ia'n ej	....	I didn't take
8	ésnad ia'j	....	I watched
9	éuoj sap ia'n ej	....	I stayed
10	étser sius ej	....	I didn't see

4 Translate these sentences into French.

1   Last year, I went to Madagascar. ....

2   I saw lots of animals yesterday. ....

3   I took more than three hundred photos. ....

> The **imperfect tense** is used to describe what you **used to do** or what things **used to be like** in the past.
>
> | | | | | |
> |---|---|---|---|---|
> | *je faisais* | I was doing / I used to do | | *j'étais* | I was |
> | *je jouais* | I was playing / I used to play | | *c'était* | it was |
> | *j'allais* | I was going / I used to go | | *il y avait* | there was / were |

G

5 Decide whether each phrase is in the perfect or imperfect tense, then translate it into English.

		perfect	imperfect	
1	j'ai fait	☐	☐	....
2	elle a dansé	☐	☐	....
3	je chantais	☐	☐	....
4	il est allé	☐	☐	....
5	il allait	☐	☐	....
6	je voyageais	☐	☐	....

1 Circle the deliberate error in each English translation, then write the corrections.

1   Elle voudrait visiter l'Algérie.   I would like to visit Algeria.   ....

2   Nice est une très grande ville.   Nice is a very small town.   ....

3   Je n'aime pas manger au resto.   I like eating out.   ....

4   Aujourd'hui, je fais un gâteau.   Today I'm making a biscuit.   ....

5   Tu vas aller à la plage?   Are you going to go to the park? ....

6   Je n'ai pas vu le film.   He didn't see the film.   ....

2 Use the words in the box to translate the sentences into English.

to the	not	a	park	I must	my	I	would like	to the	to go
national	idea	went	it's	bad	she	take	ice rink	passport	yesterday

1   Je voudrais aller au parc national.   ....

2   Ce n'est pas une mauvaise idée.   ....

3   Je dois prendre mon passeport.   ....

4   Hier, elle est allée à la patinoire.   ....

3 Translate this text into English.

> Don't just go straight to the glossary – can you use context to work out any unfamiliar words?

T

J'aimerais visiter Montréal, une grande ville au Canada. C'est une ville très impressionnante avec des monuments historiques, mais il y a beaucoup de magasins aussi. Mon prof de français est allé à Montréal l'année dernière, et il a dit qu'on doit aller au parc du Mont-Royal pour voir le coucher du soleil.

....

....

....

....

....

....

....

....

....

....

....

VERT
1 Fill in the missing words in the translations of the questions.

1 What is his name? .... s'appelle-t-il?

2 What does he do as a job? Que fait-il comme ....?

3 Where and when was he born? .... et .... est-il né?

4 What was his first success? Quel a été son .... succès?

5 What are his future plans? Quels sont ses .... d'avenir?

VERT/ROUGE
2 Translate these answers to the questions from exercise 1 into French.

1 He is called Manu Lévy. ....

2 He is a radio presenter. ....

3 He was born in Paris in 1971. ....

4 His first success was on Fun Radio. ....

....

5 He would like to work in America. ....

> *un animateur de radio*   radio presenter

ROUGE
3 Underline the English words, then rewrite the tangled text completely in French.

Manu is a radio presenter dans l'émission matinale *Manu dans le 6/9* à la radio française NRJ. C'est une radio nationale de musique contemporaine, very popular with young people. Manu works from Monday to Friday, depuis 2011. Each day, il appelle un auditeur in order to play à *Manu double votre salaire*. In the future, NRJ is going peut-être to start une émission internationale in most French-speaking countries.

....

....

....

....

....

....

....

....

Les verbes

Regular –er, –ir and –re verb patterns

Infinitive	Present tense (stem + present tense endings)	Perfect tense (avoir/être + past participle)	**R** Imperfect tense (stem + imperfect endings)	**R** Future tense (stem + future endings)
regarder to watch	je regarde tu regardes il/elle/on regarde nous regardons vous regardez ils/elles regardent	j'**ai regardé** tu **as regardé** il/elle/on **a regardé** nous **avons regardé** vous **avez regardé** ils/elles **ont regardé**	je regardais tu regardais il/elle/on regardait nous regardions vous regardiez ils/elles regardaient	je regarderai tu regarderas il/elle/on regardera nous regarderons vous regarderez ils/elles regarderont
finir to finish	je finis tu finis il/elle/on finit nous finissons vous finissez ils/elles finissent	j'**ai fini** tu **as fini** il/elle/on **a fini** nous **avons fini** vous **avez fini** ils/elles **ont fini**	je finissais tu finissais il/elle/on finissait nous finissions vous finissiez ils/elles finissaient	je finirai tu finiras il/elle/on finira nous finirons vous finirez ils/elles finiront
attendre to wait	j'attends tu attends il/elle/on attend nous attendons vous attendez ils/elles attendent	j'**ai attendu** tu **as attendu** il/elle/on **a attendu** nous **avons attendu** vous **avez attendu** ils/elles **ont attendu**	j'attendais tu attendais il/elle/on attendait nous attendions vous attendiez ils/elles attendaient	j'attendrai tu attendras il/elle/on attendra nous attendrons vous attendrez ils/elles attendront

Regular –er verb infinitives:

acheter	**to buy**	garder	**to look after**	ramasser	**to collect/pick up**
adorer	**to love**	habiter	**to live**	recycler	**to recycle**
aider	**to help**	immigrer	**to immigrate**	refuser	**to refuse**
aimer	**to like**	inventer	**to invent**	regarder	**to watch**
chanter	**to sing**	jouer	**to play**	travailler	**to work**
danser	**to dance**	manger	**to eat**	trouver	**to find**
détester	**to hate**	organiser	**to organise**	utiliser	**to use**
écouter	**to listen (to)**	porter	**to wear**	visiter	**to visit**
gagner	**to earn, to win**	protéger	**to protect**	voyager	**to travel**

Regular –ir verb infinitives:

finir	**to finish**	choisir	**to choose**	nourrir	**to feed**

Regular –re verb infinitives:

attendre	**to wait (for)**	perdre	**to lose**	entendre	**to hear**

Reflexive verbs

Infinitive	Present tense (stem + present tense endings)	Perfect tense (être + past participle)
se disputer (avec) to argue (with)	je **me** dispute tu **te** disputes il/elle/on **se** dispute nous **nous** disputons vous **vous** disputez ils/elles **se** disputent	je **me suis** disputé(e) tu **t'es** disputé(e) il/elle/on **s'est** disputé(e)(s) nous **nous sommes** disputé(e)s vous **vous êtes** disputé(e)(s) ils/elles **se sont** disputé(e)s

Remember that reflexives use être (not avoir) in the perfect tense.
Verbs that use être must agree with their subject (in gender and number).

Common reflexive verb infinitives:

s'amuser	**to enjoy yourself**	*se disputer (avec)*	**to argue (with)**	*se fâcher (contre)*	**to get angry (at)**
s'appeler	**to be called**	*se doucher*	**to shower**	*s'habiller*	**to get dressed**
se coucher	**to go to bed**	*s'entendre (avec)*	**to get on (with)**	*se laver*	**to have a wash**

Near future

To say what you are 'going to do', use the present tense of *aller* (to go) + an infinitive.

porter (to wear)	
je **vais** porter	I **am going** to wear
tu **vas** porter	you (singular) **are going** to wear
il/elle/on **va** porter	he/she **is** / we **are going** to wear
nous **allons** porter	we **are going** to wear
vous **allez** porter	you (plural or polite) **are going** to wear
ils/elles **vont** porter	they **are going** to wear

Conditional

vouloir (to want)	
je voudrais	I would like
tu voudrais	you would like
il/elle/on voudrait	he/she/we would like
nous voudrions	we would like
vous voudriez	you would like
ils/elles voudraient	they would like

R *aimer* (to like)	
j'aimerais	I would like
tu aimerais	you would like
il/elle/on aimerait	he/she/we would like
nous aimerions	we would like
vous aimeriez	you would like
ils/elles aimeraient	they would like

Key irregular verbs

Infinitive	Present tense (watch out for the change of stems)	Perfect tense (*avoir/être* + past participle)	**R** Imperfect tense (stem + imperfect endings)	**R** Future tense (watch out for the change of stems)
aller to go	je **vais** tu **vas** il/elle/on **va** nous **allons** vous **allez** ils/elles **vont**	je <u>suis</u> **allé(e)** tu <u>es</u> **allé(e)** il/elle/on <u>est</u> **allé(e)(s)** nous <u>sommes</u> **allé(e)s** vous <u>êtes</u> **allé(e)(s)** ils/elles <u>sont</u> **allé(e)s**	j'all**ais** tu all**ais** il/elle/on all**ait** nous all**ions** vous all**iez** ils/elles all**aient**	j'<u>ir</u>**ai** tu <u>ir</u>**as** il/elle/on <u>ir</u>**a** nous <u>ir</u>**ons** vous <u>ir</u>**ez** ils/elles <u>ir</u>**ont**
avoir to have	j'**ai** tu **as** il/elle/on **a** nous **avons** vous **avez** ils/elles **ont**	j'**ai eu** tu **as eu** il/elle/on **a eu** nous **avons eu** vous **avez eu** ils/elles **ont eu**	j'av**ais** tu av**ais** il/elle/on av**ait** nous av**ions** vous av**iez** ils/elles av**aient**	j'<u>aur</u>**ai** tu <u>aur</u>**as** il/elle/on <u>aur</u>**a** nous <u>aur</u>**ons** vous <u>aur</u>**ez** ils/elles <u>aur</u>**ont**
être to be	je **suis** tu **es** il/elle/on **est** nous **sommes** vous **êtes** ils/elles **sont**	j'**ai** été tu **as** été il/elle/on **a** été nous **avons** été vous **avez** été ils/elles **ont** été	j'ét**ais** tu ét**ais** il/elle/on ét**ait** nous ét**ions** vous ét**iez** ils/elles ét**aient**	je <u>ser</u>**ai** tu <u>ser</u>**as** il/elle/on <u>ser</u>**a** nous <u>ser</u>**ons** vous <u>ser</u>**ez** ils/elles <u>ser</u>**ont**
faire to do / to make	je **fais** tu **fais** il/elle/on **fait** nous **faisons** vous **faites** ils/elles **font**	j'**ai fait** tu **as fait** il/elle/on **a fait** nous **avons fait** vous **avez fait** ils/elles **ont fait**	je fais**ais** tu fais**ais** il/elle/on fais**ait** nous fais**ions** vous fais**iez** ils/elles fais**aient**	je <u>fer</u>**ai** tu <u>fer</u>**as** il/elle/on <u>fer</u>**a** nous <u>fer</u>**ons** vous <u>fer</u>**ez** ils/elles <u>fer</u>**ont**

Les verbes

Other useful irregular verbs

Infinitive	Present tense (watch out for the change of stems)	Perfect tense (avoir/être + past participle)	Ⓡ Imperfect tense (stem + imperfect endings)	Ⓡ Future tense (watch out for the change of stems)
boire to drink	je **bois** tu **bois** il/elle/on **boit** nous **buvons** vous **buvez** ils/elles **boivent**	j'**ai bu** tu **as bu** il/elle/on **a bu** nous **avons bu** vous **avez bu** ils/elles **ont bu**	je buv**ais** tu buv**ais** il/elle/on buv**ait** nous buv**ions** vous buv**iez** ils/elles buv**aient**	je boir**ai** tu boir**as** il/elle/on boir**a** nous boir**ons** vous boir**ez** ils/elles boir**ont**
lire to read	je **lis** tu **lis** il/elle/on **lit** nous **lisons** vous **lisez** ils/elles **lisent**	j'**ai lu** tu **as lu** il/elle/on **a lu** nous **avons lu** vous **avez lu** ils/elles **ont lu**	je lis**ais** tu lis**ais** il/elle/on lis**ait** nous lis**ions** vous lis**iez** ils/elles lis**aient**	je lir**ai** tu lir**as** il/elle/on lir**a** nous lir**ons** vous lir**ez** ils/elles lir**ont**
ouvrir to open	j'**ouvre** tu **ouvres** il/elle/on **ouvre** nous **ouvrons** vous **ouvrez** ils/elles **ouvrent**	j'**ai ouvert** tu **as ouvert** il/elle/on **a ouvert** nous **avons ouvert** vous **avez ouvert** ils/elles **ont ouvert**	j'ouvr**ais** tu ouvr**ais** il/elle/on ouvr**ait** nous ouvr**ions** vous ouvr**iez** ils/elles ouvr**aient**	j'ouvrir**ai** tu ouvrir**as** il/elle/on ouvrir**a** nous ouvrir**ons** vous ouvrir**ez** ils/elles ouvrir**ont**
voir to see	je **vois** tu **vois** il/elle/on **voit** nous **voyons** vous **voyez** ils/elles **voient**	j'**ai vu** tu **as vu** il/elle/on **a vu** nous **avons vu** vous **avez vu** ils/elles **ont vu**	je voy**ais** tu voy**ais** il/elle/on voy**ait** nous voy**ions** vous voy**iez** ils/elles voy**aient**	je <u>verr</u>**ai** tu <u>verr</u>**as** il/elle/on <u>verr</u>**a** nous <u>verr</u>**ons** vous <u>verr</u>**ez** ils/elles <u>verr</u>**ont**

Modals are key irregular verbs. They're followed by an infinitive.

Infinitive	Present tense (watch out for the change of stems)	Perfect tense (avoir/être + past participle)	Ⓡ Imperfect tense (stem + imperfect endings)	Ⓡ Future tense (infinitive + future endings)
devoir to have to (must)	je **dois** tu **dois** il/elle/on **doit** nous **devons** vous **devez** ils/elles **doivent**	j'**ai dû** tu **as dû** il/elle/on **a dû** nous **avons dû** vous **avez dû** ils/elles **ont dû**	je dev**ais** tu dev**ais** il/elle/on dev**ait** nous dev**ions** vous dev**iez** ils/elles dev**aient**	je <u>devr</u>**ai** tu <u>devr</u>**as** il/elle/on <u>devr</u>**a** nous <u>devr</u>**ons** vous <u>devr</u>**ez** ils/elles <u>devr</u>**ont**
pouvoir to be able to (can)	je **peux** tu **peux** il/elle/on **peut** nous **pouvons** vous **pouvez** ils/elles **peuvent**	j'**ai pu** tu **as pu** il/elle/on **a pu** nous **avons pu** vous **avez pu** ils/elles **ont pu**	je pouv**ais** tu pouv**ais** il/elle/on pouv**ait** nous pouv**ions** vous pouv**iez** ils/elles pouv**aient**	je <u>pourr</u>**ai** tu <u>pourr</u>**as** il/elle/on <u>pourr</u>**a** nous <u>pourr</u>**ons** vous <u>pourr</u>**ez** ils/elles <u>pourr</u>**ont**
vouloir to want to	je **veux** tu **veux** il/elle/on **veut** nous **voulons** vous **voulez** ils/elles **veulent**	j'**ai voulu** tu **as voulu** il/elle/on **a voulu** nous **avons voulu** vous **avez voulu** ils/elles **ont voulu**	je voul**ais** tu voul**ais** il/elle/on voul**ait** nous voul**ions** vous voul**iez** ils/elles voul**aient**	je <u>voudr</u>**ai** tu <u>voudr</u>**as** il/elle/on <u>voudr</u>**a** nous <u>voudr</u>**ons** vous <u>voudr</u>**ez** ils/elles <u>voudr</u>**ont**

A

à cause de *because of*
l' **accès** *(m)* *access*
actuellement *currently*
l' **abonné** *(m)* *subscriber*
à côté *alongside*
à droite *on the right*
à gauche *on the left*
à l'étranger *abroad*
à la maison *at home*
à pied *by/on foot*
à vélo *by bike*
acheter *(v)* *to buy*
l' **activité** *(f)* **extrascolaire** *after-school activity*
adorer *(v)* *to love*
l' **adulte** *(m/f)* *adult*
l' **Afrique** *(f)* *Africa*
affreux(–se) *(adj)* *awful*
l' **âge** *(m)* *age*
aider *(v)* *to help*
aimer *(v)* *to like*
l' **albatros** *(m)* **hurleur** *wandering albatross*
l' **album** *(m)* *album*
l' **Algérie** *(f)* *Algeria*
aller *(v)* **en ville** *to go in to town*
les **Alpes** *(f.pl)* *the Alps*
l' **Amérique** *(f)* **du Sud** *South America*
l' **ami(e)** *friend*
amusant(e) *(adj)* *fun*
s'amuser *(v)* *to enjoy yourself*
l' **an** *(m)* *year*
l' **anglais** *(m)* *English*
l' **Angleterre** *(f)* *England*
l' **animal** *(m)* *animal*
les **animaux** *(m.pl)* *animals*
l' **année** *(f)* *year*
l' **anniversaire** *(m)* *birthday*
l' **appartement** *(m)* *apartment; flat*
s'appeler *(v)* *to be called*
apprendre *(v)* **(à)** *to learn (how) (to)*
apporter *(v)* *to provide; to bring*
après *after; afterwards*
l' **après-midi** *(m, f)* *afternoon*
l' **araignée** *(f)* *spider*
l' **architecte** *(m/f)* *architect*
l' **argent** *(m)* *money*
arrêter *(v)* *to stop*
arrogant(e) *(adj)* *arrogant*
l' **artiste** *(m/f)* *artist*
l' **Asie** *(f)* *Asia*
assez *quite*
au centre *in the centre*
au fond *at the back*
aujourd'hui *today*
aussi *also*
l' **auteur** *(m)* *author*
les **autres** *(m.pl)* *others*
avant *before*
avec **(qui)** *with (whom)*
l' **avenir** *(m)* *future*
l' **avis** *(m)* *opinion; mind*
avoir *(v)* **raison** *to be right*
avoir *(v)* **tort** *to be wrong*

B

le **baby-sitting** *babysitting*
le **bac de recyclage** *recycling bin*
le **badminton** *badminton*
la **banque** *bank*
les **baskets** *(f.pl)* *trainers*
le **bateau** *boat*
le **bâtiment** *building*
la **batterie** *drums*
la **BD** *comic*
beau, belle *(adj)* *beautiful*
beaucoup **(de)** *lots of; a lot (of)*
bête *(adj)* *stupid*
bien *well*
bien sûr *of course*
le **billet (de cinéma)** *(cinema) ticket*
bio *(adj)* *organic*
blanc(he) *(adj)* *white*
bleu(e) *(adj)* *blue*
le **blog** *blog*
bloguer *(v)* *to blog*
blond(e) *(adj)* *blond, blonde*
boire *(v)* *to drink*
bon(ne) *(adj)* *good*
le **bonbon** *sweet*
la **botte** *boot*
bouclé(e) *(adj)* *curly*
le **boulot** *job; work*
la **bouteille** *bottle*
le **bowling** *bowling*
britannique *(adj)* *British*
se bronzer *(v)* *to sunbathe*
brun(e) *(adj)* *brown*
le **bureau** *office*
le **but** *goal*

C

ça *that; it*
le **cadeau** *present; gift*
le **café** *coffee; café*
le **cahier** *exercise book*
la **caméra** *camera*
la **campagne** *campaign; country(side)*
le **Canada** *Canada*
la **cantine** *canteen*
car *because*
caritatif(–ve) *(adj)* *charitable*
carnassier(–ère) *(adj)* *carnivorous*
les **cartes** *(f.pl)* *cards*
la **casquette** *cap*
la **cassette audio** *audio cassette*
la **cathédrale** *cathedral*
le **CD** *CD*
célèbre *(adj)* *famous*
cent *(a) hundred*
le **centre commercial** *shopping centre*
le **centre de recyclage** *recycling centre*
cependant *however*
les **céréales** *(f.pl)* *cereal(s); grains*

la **chaîne web** *internet channel*
la **chambre** *(bed)room*
changer *(v)* *to change*
la **chanson** *song*
chanter *(v)* *to sing*
le **chanteur** *singer (m)*
la **chanteuse** *singer (f)*
le **chapeau** *hat*
chaque *each; every*
le **changement** *change*
la **chasse** *hunting*
le **chat** *cat*
le **château** *castle*
la **chaussette** *sock*
la **chaussure** *shoe*
la **chemise** *shirt*
cher (chère) *(adj)* *expensive; dear*
chercher *(v)* *to look for*
les **cheveux** *(m.pl)* *hair*
chez Google *at Google*
le **chien** *dog*
la **Chine** *China*
les **chips** *(f.pl)* *crisps*
le **chocolat** *chocolate*
choisir *(v)* *to choose*
la **chorale** *choir*
la **chose** *thing*
chouette *(adj)* *nice*
le **cinéma** *cinema*
la **clarinette** *clarinette*
classé(e) *(adj)* *classed*
le **clavier** *keyboard*
le(s) **clip(s) vidéo** *video clip(s)*
climatique *(adj)* *climate (adj)*
le **club (de danse)** *(dance) club*
le **coca** *cola*
le **collège** *secondary school*
combattre *(v)* *to fight; to combat*
combien de *how many; how much*
comme *like; as*
commencer *(v)* *to begin; to start*
la **compétition** *competition*
complètement *completely*
le **concert** *concert*
conserver *(v)* *to conserve*
consommer *(v)* *to consume*
contemporain(e) *(adj)* *contemporary*
continuer **(à)** *to continue (to)*
contre *against*
cool *(adj)* *cool*
le **coucher du soleil** *sunset*
le **copain** *friend (m)*
la **copine** *friend (f)*
le **costume** *suit; costume*
le(s) **cours** *lesson(s)*
court(e) *(adj)* *short*
la **cravate** *tie*
créatif(–ve) *(adj)* *creative*
créer *(v)* *to create*
la **Croatie** *Croatia*
le **cuir** *leather*
la **cuisine** *kitchen; cooking*
cuisiner *(v)* *to cook*
le **cuisinier** *(m)* *cook (m)*
la **cuisinière** *(f)* *cook (f)*
la **culture** *culture*

Glossaire (français – anglais)

D

d'abord *first of all*
d'accord *in agreement*
dangereux(–se) *(adj)* *dangerous*
dans *in*
la danse *dancing*
danser *(v)* *to dance*
le danseur *dancer (m)*
la danseuse *dancer (f)*
de luxe *deluxe; luxury*
de taille moyenne *middle-sized*
de temps en temps *from time to time*
les déchets *(m.pl)* *rubbish*
décider *(v)* (de) *to decide (to)*
la déforestation *deforestation*
le déjeuner *lunch*
délicieux(–se) *(adj)* *delicious*
demain *tomorrow*
demain soir *tomorrow evening*
démodé(e) *(adj)* *old-fashioned*
depuis *since; from*
dernier(–ère) *(adj)* *last*
derrière (elle/lui) *behind (him/her)*
le dessin *art*
le dessin animé *cartoon*
dessiner *(v)* *to draw*
la destination *destination*
détester *(v)* *to hate*
deux (fois) *two (times/twice)*
développer *(v)* *to develop*
devenir *(v)* *to become*
devoir *(v)* *to have to (must)*
les devoirs *(m.pl)* *homework*
d'ici (… ans) *(… years) from now*
différent(e) *(adj)* *different*
difficile *(adj)* *difficult*
dimanche *Sunday*
dire *(v)* *to say*
se disputer (avec) *to argue (with)*
dix *ten*
donner *(v)* *to give*
dormir *(v)* *to sleep*
se doucher *(v)* *to have a shower*
drôle *(adj)* *funny*
le drone *drone*
dur(e) *(adj)* *hard*

E

l' eau *(f)* *water*
l' école *(f)* (primaire) *(primary) school*
les économies *(f.pl)* *savings*
écouter *(v)* *to listen to*
écrire *(v)* *to write*
effrayant(e) *(adj)* *frightening*
efficace *(adj)* *effective; efficient*
l' église *(f)* *church*
électrique *(adj)* *electric*
l' éléphant *(m)* *elephant*
l' élève *(m/f)* *pupil*
l' émission *(f)* *programme*
l' emploi *(m)* du temps *timetable*
l' empreinte *(f)* carbone *carbon footprint*
emprunter *(v)* *to borrow*
en général *in general*

l' énergie *(f)* *energy*
l' enfant *(m/f)* *child*
les enfants *(m/f.pl)* *children*
ennuyeux(–se) *(adj)* *boring*
ensemble *together*
ensuite *next*
s'entendre *(v)* (bien) avec *to get on (well) with*
s'entraîner *(v)* *to train*
entrer *(v)* (dans) *to enter*
l' environnement *environment*
l' EPS *(f)* *PE*
équilibré(e) *(adj)* *balanced*
l' équipe (nationale) *(national) team*
l' Espagne *(f)* *Spain*
essayer *(v)* (de) *to try (to)*
et *and*
les États-Unis *(m.pl)* *United States (of America)*
l' été *summer*
être *(v)* *to be*
étudier *(v)* *to study*
examiner *(v)* *to examine*
l' excursion *(f)* *excursion*
extraordinaire *(adj)* *extraordinary*

F

fabuleux(–se) *(adj)* *fabulous*
se fâcher *(v)* (contre) *to get angry (with)*
facile *(adj)* *easy*
la famille *family*
fantastique *(adj)* *fantastic*
fatigant(e) *(adj)* *tiring*
la femme *woman; wife*
la fête *party*
fêter *(v)* *to celebrate*
fier (fière) *(adj)* *proud*
la fille *girl; daughter*
le film *film*
finalement *finally*
finir *(v)* *to finish*
la fleur *flower*
la flûte *flute*
la fois *time (une fois=one time/once)*
le footing *jogging*
la forêt (tropicale) *(tropical) forest*
la formation *training*
la fraise *strawberry*
le Français *French person (m)*
la Française *French person (f)*
la France *France*
francophone *(adj)* *francophone; French-speaking*
le frère *brother*
frisé(e) *(adj)* *very curly*
les frites *(f.pl)* *chips*
le fromage *cheese*
la frontière *border*
le fruit *(piece of) fruit*
les fruits *(m.pl)* de mer *seafood*
furieux(–se) *(adj)* *furious*

G

gagner *(v)* *to win; to earn*
le garçon *boy*
garder *(v)* *to look after*
le gâteau *cake*
géant(e) *giant*
génial(e) *(adj)* *great*
gentil(le) *kind*
la glace *ice cream*
grand(e) *(adj)* *big; tall*
gris(e) *(adj)* *grey*
la grotte *cave*
le groupe (d'amis) *group (of friends)*
le groupe écologique *green group*
le guépard *cheetah*
la guitare *guitar*
la gymnastique *gymnastics*

H

s'habiller *to get dressed*
habiter *(v)* *to live*
le hard rock *hard rock*
le haricot *bean*
haut(e) *(adj)* *high*
l' heure *(f)* *o'clock; hour*
l' heure *(f)* du déjeuner *lunchtime*
heureusement *fortunately*
heureux(–se) *(adj)* *happy*
hier *yesterday*
le hip-hop *hip-hop*
l' histoire-géo *(f)* *history and geography*
historique *(adj)* *historic*
l' homme *(m)* *man*
l' hôpital *(m)* *hospital*

I

ici *here*
l' idée *(f)* *idea*
il y a *there is/are*
il y a … ans *… years ago*
il y aura *there will be*
il y avait *there was/were*
l' île *(f)* *island*
l' image *(f)* *image; picture*
immigrer *(v)* *to immigrate*
impatient(e) *(adj)* *impatient*
important(e) *(adj)* *important*
impressionnant(e) *(adj)* *impressive*
incroyable *(adj)* *incredible*
l' infirmier *(m)* *nurse (m)*
l' infirmière *(f)* *nurse (f)*
l' ingénieur *(m)* *engineer (m)*
l' ingénieure *(f)* *engineer (f)*
l' instituteur *(m)* *primary school teacher (m)*
l' institutrice *(f)* *primary school teacher (f)*
l' instrument *(m)* *instrument*
intéressant(e) *(adj)* *interesting*
inventer *(v)* *to invent*
l' inventeur *(m)* *inventor (m)*
l' inventrice *(f)* *inventor (f)*
inviter *(v)* *to invite*

J

le **jardin** garden
jaune (adj) yellow
le **jazz** jazz
le **jean** jeans
jeune (adj) young
le/la **jeune** young person
les **Jeux** (m. pl) **Olympiques** Olympic Games
le **jeu(x) vidéo** video game(s)
joli(e) (adj) pretty
jouer (v) (à / de) to play
le **jour** (m) day
le **journal** newspaper
journalier(–ère) daily
la **journée** day
la **jupe** skirt
juste fair; just

K

le **karting** go-carting

L

le **lac** lake
laid(e) (adj) ugly
laisser (v) to leave
le **lait** milk
la **langue** language
le **lapin** rabbit
laver to wash
se laver les dents to clean your teeth
la **lecture** reading
le **légume** vegetable
se lever to get up
la **ligne (en ligne)** line (online)
la **limonade** lemonade
lire (v) to read
le **lit** bed
la **livraison** delivery
loger to stay
Londres London
long(ue) (adj) long
lui him
lundi Monday
la **Lune** moon
les **lunettes** (f.pl) glasses
le **Luxembourg** Luxembourg
le **lycée** sixth form (college)

M

le **magasin** shop
magnifique (adj) magnificent
maintenant now
mais but
la **maison** house
le **mammifère** mammal
manger (v) to eat
le **maquillage** make-up; cosmetics
le **marché** market
marié(e) (adj) married
marin(e) (adj) sea (adj)

marquer (v) to score (goal)
marron (adj) brown
le **match** match
les **maths** (f.pl) maths
la **matière** (school) subject
le **matin** morning
mauvais(e) (adj) bad
le **mécanicien** mechanic (m)
la **mécanicienne** mechanic (f)
méchant(e) (adj) naughty
la **médaille** medal
meilleur(e) (adj) best; better
la **mélodie** melody; tune
le **melon** melon
le **membre** member
menacé(e) (adj) endangered; threatened
la **mer** sea
la **mère** mother
mercredi Wednesday
le **message** message
le **métier** job
mettre (v) to put on
midi midday
mignon(ne) (adj) cute
mi-long(ue) (adj) mid-length
moi me
moderne (adj) modern
moins less; fewer
le **monde** world
le **mont** mount
la **montagne** mountain
le **monument (historique)** (historic) monument
le **musée (d'art)** museum (of art)
le **musicien** (m) musician (m)
la **musicienne** (f) musician (f)
la **musique (classique)** (classical) music
mystérieux(–se) (adj) mysterious

N

nager (v) to swim
national(e) (adj) national
ne … jamais never
ne … rien nothing
ne … pas not
né(e) (adj) born
nettoyer (v) to clean
noir(e) (adj) black
nourrir (v) to feed
nouveau(–elle) (adj) new
nul(le) (adj) rubbish

O

l' **orchestre** (m) orchestra
l' **ordinateur** (m) computer
l' **organisation** (f) **caritative** charity; charitable organisation
organiser (v) to organise
original(e) (adj) original
ou or
où where
l' **ouest** (m) west
ouvrir (v) to open

P

le **pain** bread
le **pantalon** trousers
le **papier** paper
parfois sometimes
le **parc aquatique** water park
le **parc national** national park
parce que because
paresseux(–se) lazy
parler (v) to speak
les **paroles** (f.pl) lyrics; words
participer (v) (à) to participate (in)
pas du tout not at all
le **passeport** passport
passer (v) **du temps avec** to spend time with
passionnant(e) (adj) exciting
patient(e) (adj) patient
la **patinoire** ice skating rink
le **pays** country
pendant during; for (e.g. an hour)
penser (v) to think
le **père** father
le **petit boulot** part-time job
petit(e) (adj) small
le **petit copain** boyfriend
la **petite copine** girlfriend
un **peu** a bit
peut-être perhaps
la **photo** photo
le **piano** piano
le **pied** foot
le/la **pilote** pilot
la **piscine** swimming pool
la **pizza** pizza
la **plage** beach
la **planète** planet
le **plastique (à usage unique)** (single-use) plastic
pleuvoir (v) to rain
la **plupart de** most (of)
plus more
plus tard later
le **poisson** fish
le **policier** police officer (m)
la **policière** police officer (f)
polluer (v) to pollute
la **pomme** apple
le **pont** bridge
le **popcorn** popcorn
populaire (adj) popular
le **portable** (mobile) phone
porter (v) to wear
le **portugais** Portuguese
poster (v) to post (online)
le **poulet** chicken
pour moi for me
pour in order to; for
pourquoi why
préféré(e) (adj) favourite
préférer (v) to prefer
premier first
prendre (v) to take
présenter (v) to present

le **prix** *prize*
prochain(e) *(adj)* *next*
le **produit (d'origine animale)** *(animal) product*
les **produits** *(m.pl)* **laitiers** *milk/dairy products*
le **professeur** *teacher*
professionnel(le) *(adj)* *professional*
progresser *(v)* *to progress*
les **projets** *(m.pl)* *plans*
la **promenade** *walk*
protéger *(v)* *to protect*
puis *then*
le **pull** *jumper*

Q

que/qu' *what; than*
quand *when*
quelque chose *something*
qui *who*
quitter *(v)* *to leave*

R

le **R'n'B** *R'n'B*
la **radio** *radio*
raide *(adj)* *straight*
ramasser *(v)* *to collect; to pick up*
la **randonnée** *hike; walk*
ranger *(v)* *to tidy (up)*
le **rap** *rap*
rapide *(adj)* *fast*
récemment *recently*
recevoir *(v)* *to receive*
la **récré** *break-time*
recycler *(v)* *to recycle*
réduire *(v)* *to reduce*
refuser *(v)* *to refuse*
regarder *(v)* *to watch*
le **reggae** *reggae*
la **région** *region*
rencontrer *(v)* *to meet*
rentrer *(v)* *to go home*
le **repas** *meal*
se reposer *(v)* *to rest*
respecter *(v)* *to respect*
le **restaurant** *restaurant*
rester *(v)* *to stay; to remain*
le **resto** *restaurant*
retrouver *(v)* *to meet up with*
réutilisable *(adj)* *reuseable*
riche *(adj)* *rich*
rigoler *(v)* *to have a laugh*
rigolo *(adj)* *funny; a laugh*
la **rivière** *river*
le **riz** *rice*
la **robe** *dress*
le **robot** *robot*
le **roman** *novel*
romantique *romantic*
rose *(adj)* *pink*
rouge *(adj)* *red*
roux *(adj)* *red; ginger (e.g. hair)*
le **rugby** *rugby*
le **rythme** *rhythm*

S

le **sac (en plastique)** *(plastic) bag*
sain(e) *(adj)* *healthy*
la **salade** *salad*
samedi *Saturday*
sans *without*
sauf *except*
savoureux(–se) *(adj)* *tasty*
les **sciences** *(f.pl)* *science*
le/la **scientifique** *scientist*
le **selfie** *selfie*
la **semaine** *week*
le **Sénégal** *Senegal*
le **sens de l'humour** *sense of humour*
seul(e) *(adj)* *alone*
sévère *(adj)* *strict*
les **Seychelles** *(f.pl)* *Seychelles*
simple *(adj)* *simple*
le **site (historique)** *(historic) site*
le **site web** *website*
situé(e) *(adj)* *situated*
le **snowboard** *snowboarding*
la **sœur** *sister*
le **soir** *evening*
sortir *(v)* *to go out*
la **soupe** *soup*
le **souvenir (d'origine animale)** *souvenir (made from animal products)*
souvent *often*
la **spécialité** *speciality*
le **sport** *sport*
le **stade** *stadium*
le **succès** *success*
le **sud** *south*
la **Suisse** *Switzerland*
super *(adj)* *super*
le **supermarché** *supermarket*
sur *on*
le **surfeur** *surfer (m)*
la **surfeuse** *surfer (f)*
surfer *(v)* *to surf*
surtout *especially*
le **sweat** *sweatshirt*
le **sweat à capuche** *hoodie*
sympa *(adj)* *nice; friendly*

T

de taille moyenne *medium height*
tard *late*
tchatter *(v)* *to chat (online)*
la **techno** *techno music*
le **tee-shirt** *tee-shirt*
tellement *particularly*
le **temple** *temple*
le **temps** *time; weather*
le **théâtre** *theatre*
le **tigre** *tiger*
timide *(adj)* *shy*
tomber *(v)* *to fall*
la **tortue** *tortoise*
la **tortue marine** *turtle*
toujours *always*
la **tour** *tower*

le **tour (du monde)** *(world) tour*
le/la **touriste** *tourist*
tous les jours *every day*
tout *everything*
toutes sortes de *all sorts of*
le **travail (bénévole)** *(voluntary) work*
travailler *(v)* *to work*
très *very*
la **trompette** *trumpet*
trop *too; too much/many*
trouver *(v)* *to find*
la **Tunisie** *Tunisia*

U

unique *(adj)* *unique*
utile *(adj)* *useful*
utiliser *(v)* *to use*
l' **université** *(f)* *university*

V

les **vacances** *(f.pl)* *holiday(s)*
la **vache** *cow*
la **vaisselle** *washing-up*
varié(e) *(adj)* *varied*
végétarien(ne) *(adj)* *vegetarian*
le **végétarisme** *vegetarianism*
le **vélo** *bicycle; cycling*
vendredi *Friday*
vert(e) *(adj)* *green*
la **veste** *jacket; blazer*
les **vêtements** *(m.pl)* *clothes*
le/la **vétérinaire** *vet*
la **viande** *meat*
vieux (vieille) *(adj)* *old*
le **village** *village*
la **ville** *town*
violet(te) *(adj)* *purple*
le **violon** *violin*
virtuel(le) *(adj)* *virtual*
la **visite (guidée)** *(guided) visit*
visiter *(v)* *to visit*
voici *here is/are*
voir *to see*
le/la **voisin(e)** *neighbour*
la **voiture** *car*
voyager *(v)* *to travel*
vraiment *really*
la **vue** *view*
vulnérable *(adj)* *vulnerable; at risk*

W

le **weekend** *weekend*

Y

les **yeux** *(m.pl)* *eyes*

A

a bit	un peu
abroad	à l'étranger
access	l'accès (m)
adult	l'adulte (m/f)
Africa	l'Afrique (f)
after(wards)	après
afternoon	l'après-midi (m, f)
after-school activity	l'activité (f) extrascolaire
against	contre
age	l'âge (m)
ago, (ten) years	il y a (dix) ans
agree (v)	être (m) d'accord
all sorts of	toutes sortes de
alone (adj)	seul(e)
alongside	à côté
Alps, the	les Alpes (f.pl)
also	aussi
always	toujours
and	et
animal(s)	l'animal (m); les animaux
animal product	le produit d'origine animale
apartment	l'appartement (m)
apple	la pomme
architect	l'architecte (m/f)
argue (v) (with)	se disputer (v) (avec)
art	le dessin
artist	l'artiste (m/f)
Asia	l'Asie (f)
at Google	chez Google
at home	à la maison
at risk	vulnérable (adj)
awful (adj)	affreux(–se)

B

babysitting	le baby-sitting
back, at the	au fond
bad (adj)	mauvais(e)
bag	le sac
balanced (adj)	équilibré(e)
be (v)	être
beach	la plage
bean	le haricot
beautiful (adj)	beau, belle
because	parce que; car
because of	à cause de
become (v)	devenir
bedroom	la chambre
before	avant
begin (v)	commencer
behind (him/her)	derrière (elle/lui)
Belgium	la Belgique
best (adj)	meilleur(e)
better (adj)	meilleur(e)
bicycle	le vélo
big (adj)	grand(e)
birthday	l'anniversaire (m)
black (adj)	noir(e)
blazer	la veste
blog	le blog

blog (v)	bloguer
blond(e) (adj)	blond(e)
blue (adj)	bleu(e)
boat	le bateau
boot	la botte
border	la frontière
boring (adj)	ennuyeux(–se)
born (adj)	né(e)
borrow (v)	emprunter
bottle	la bouteille
bowling	le bowling
boy	le garçon
boyfriend	le petit copain
bread	le pain
break-time	la récré
bridge	le pont
bring (v)	apporter
British (adj)	britannique
brother	le frère
brown (adj)	brun(e); marron
building	le bâtiment
but	mais
buy (v)	acheter
by bike	à vélo
by foot	à pied

C

café	le café
cake	le gâteau
called, to be (v)	s'appeler
camera	la caméra
campaign	la campagne
Canada	le Canada
canteen	la cantine
cap	la casquette
car	la voiture
carbon footprint	l'empreinte (f) carbone
carnivorous (adj)	carnassier(–ère)
cartoon	le dessin animé
castle	le château
cat	le chat
cathedral	la cathédrale
CD	le CD
celebrate (v)	fêter
centre, in the	au centre
cereal(s)	les céréales (f.pl)
change	le changement
change (v)	changer
charity	l'organisation (f) caritative
chat (v) (online)	tchatter
cheese	le fromage
cheetah	le guépard
chicken	le poulet
children	les enfants (m/f.pl)
China	la Chine
chips	les frites (f.pl)
chocolate	le chocolat
choir	la chorale
choose (v)	choisir
church	l'église (f)
cinema	le cinéma
clarinette	la clarinette
classical music	la musique classique

clean (v)	nettoyer
clean (v) your teeth	se laver les dents
climate (adj)	climatique
clothes	les vêtements (m.pl)
club	le club
coffee	le café
cola	le coca
collect (v)	ramasser
combat (v)	combattre
comic	la BD
competition	la compétition
completely	complètement
computer	l'ordinateur (m)
contemporary (adj)	contemporain(e)
concert	le concert
conserve (v)	conserver
consume (v)	consommer
continue (v) (to)	continuer (v) (à)
cook	le/la cuisinier(–ère)
cook (v)	cuisiner
cooking	la cuisine
cool (adj)	cool
country	le pays
country(side)	la campagne
cow	la vache
create (v)	créer
creative (adj)	créatif(–ve)
crisps	les chips (f.pl)
curly (adj)	bouclé(e)
currently	actuellement
cute (adj)	mignon(ne)
cycling	le vélo

D

daily	journalier(–ère)
dairy products	les produits (m.pl) laitiers
dance (v)	danser
dancer	le/la danseur(–se)
dancing	la danse
dangerous (adj)	dangereux(–se)
daughter	la fille
day	le jour; la journée
dear (adj)	cher (chère)
decide (v) (to)	décider (v) (de)
deforestation	la déforestation
delicious (adj)	délicieux(–se)
delivery	la livraison
destination	la destination
develop (v)	développer
different (adj)	différent(e)
difficult (adj)	difficile
dog	le chien
draw (v)	dessiner
dress	la robe
drink (v)	boire
drums	la batterie
during	pendant

E

each	chaque
earn (v)	gagner

Glossaire (anglais – français)

easy (adj)	facile	frightening (adj)	effrayant(e)	holiday(s)	les vacances (f.pl)
eat (v)	manger	(… years)	d'ici (… ans)	homework	les devoirs (m.pl)
effective (adj)	efficace	from now		hoodie	le sweat à capuche
electric (adj)	électrique	from time	de temps en temps	hospital	l'hôpital (m)
elephant	l'éléphant (m)	to time		hour	l'heure (f)
endangered	menacé(e)	fruit (piece of)	le fruit	house	la maison
(adj)		fun (adj)	amusant(e)	how many/	combien de
energy	l'énergie (f)	funny (adj)	drôle; rigolo	much	
engineer	l'ingénieur(e)	furious (adj)	furieux(–se)	however	cependant
England	l'Angleterre (f)	future	l'avenir (m)	(a) hundred	cent
English	l'anglais (m)			hunting	la chasse
enjoy (v)	s'amuser	**G**			
yourself		garden	le jardin	**I**	
enter (v)	entrer (v) (dans)	get (v) angry	se fâcher (v)	ice cream	la glace
environment	l'environnement	(with)	(contre)	ice skating rink	la patinoire
especially	surtout	get (v) dressed	s'habiller	idea	l'idée (f)
evening	le soir	get (v) up	se lever	image	l'image (f)
every	chaque	get (v) on	s'entendre (v)	immigrate (v)	immigrer
every day	tous les jours	(well) with	(bien) avec	impatient (adj)	impatient(e)
everything	tout (m)	giant (adj)	géant(e)	important (adj)	important(e)
examine (v)	examiner	gift	le cadeau	impressive (adj)	impressionnant(e)
except	sauf	ginger (e.g. hair)	roux (–sse)	in	dans
exciting (adj)	passionnant(e)	(adj)		in general	en général
excursion	l'excursion (f)	girl	la fille	in order to	pour
exercise book	le cahier	girlfriend	la petite copine	incredible (adj)	incroyable
expensive (adj)	cher (chère)	give (v)	donner	instrument	l'instrument (m)
extraordinary	extraordinaire	glasses	les lunettes (f.pl)	interesting (adj)	intéressant(e)
(adj)		go (v) home	rentrer	internet channel	la chaîne web
eyes	les yeux (m.pl)	go (v) in	aller (v) en ville	invent (v)	inventer
		to town		inventor	l'inventeur(–rice)
F		go (v) out	sortir	invite (v)	inviter
fabulous (adj)	fabuleux(–se)	go-carting	le karting	island	l'île (f)
fair	juste	good (adj)	bon(ne)		
fall (v)	tomber	great (adj)	génial(e)	**J**	
family	la famille	green (adj)	vert(e)	jacket	la veste
famous (adj)	célèbre	green group	le groupe	jazz	le jazz
fantastic (adj)	fantastique		écologique	jeans	le jean
fast (adj)	rapide	grey (adj)	gris(e)	job	le métier; le boulot
father	le père	group (of	le groupe (d'amis)	jogging	le footing
favourite (adj)	préféré(e)	friends)		jumper	le pull
fewer	moins	guitar	la guitare	just	juste
fight (v)	combattre	gymnastics	la gymnastique		
film	le film			**K**	
finally	finalement	**H**		keyboard	le clavier
find (v)	trouver	hair	les cheveux (m.pl)	kind (adj)	gentil(le)
finish (v)	finir	happy (adj)	heureux(–se)	kitchen	la cuisine
first	premier	hard (adj)	dur(e)		
first of all	d'abord	hat	le chapeau	**L**	
fish	le poisson	hate (v)	détester	lake	le lac
flower	la fleur	have (v) a	se doucher	language	la langue
flute	la flûte	shower		last (adj)	dernier(–ère)
foot	le pied	have to (v)	devoir	late	tard
for (moi)	pour (moi)	(must)		later	plus tard
for (e.g. an	pendant	healthy (adj)	sain(e)	lazy (adj)	paresseux(–se)
hour)		help (v)	aider	learn (v)	apprendre (v) (à)
forest	la forêt	here	ici	(how) (to)	
fortunately	heureusement	here is/are	voici	leather	le cuir
France	la France	high (adj)	haut(e)	leave (v) (thing)	laisser
French	le/la Français(e)	hike	la randonnée	leave (v) (place)	quitter
person		him	lui	left, on the	à gauche
French-speaking	francophone	hip-hop	le hip-hop	lemonade	la limonade
(adj)		historic (adj)	historique	less	moins
Friday	vendredi	history and	l'histoire-géo (f)		
friend	l'ami(e)	geography			
friend	le copain/la copine				

Dynamo 3 © Pearson Education Ltd 2020

lesson(s)	le(s) cours	neighbour	le/la voisin(e)	popular (adj)	populaire
like (v)	aimer	never	ne … jamais	Portuguese	le portugais
like; as	comme	new (adj)	nouveau(–elle)	post (v) (online)	poster
listen (v) to	écouter	newspaper	le journal	prefer (v)	préférer
live (v)	habiter	next	ensuite	present	le cadeau
London	Londres	next (adj)	prochain(e)	present (v)	présenter
long (adj)	long(ue)	nice (adj)	chouette; sympa	pretty (adj)	joli(e)
look (v) after	garder	not	ne … pas	primary school	l'école (f) primaire
look (v) for	chercher	not at all	pas du tout	prize	le prix
lots of; a lot (of)	beaucoup (de)	nothing	ne … rien	product	le produit
love (v)	adorer	novel	le roman	professional	professionnel(le)
lunch	le déjeuner	now	maintenant	(adj)	
lunchtime	l'heure (f) du	nurse	l'infirmier(–ère)	programme	l'émission (f)
	déjeuner			progress (v)	progresser
Luxembourg	le Luxembourg			protect (v)	protéger
luxury	de luxe			proud (adj)	fier (fière)
lyrics (words)	les paroles (f.pl)			provide (v)	apporter

M

O

		o'clock	l'heure (f)	pupil	l'élève (m/f)
magnificent	magnifique	of course	bien sûr	put (v) on	mettre
(adj)		office	le bureau		
make-up	le maquillage	often	souvent		
man	l'homme (m)	old (adj)	vieux (vieille)		
market	le marché	old-fashioned	démodé(e)		

Q

married (adj)	marié(e)	(adj)		quite	assez
match	le match	Olympic Games	les Jeux (m. pl)		
maths	les maths (f.pl)		Olympiques		
me	moi	on	sur		

R

meal	le repas	on foot	à pied	R'n'B	le R'n'B
meat	la viande	online	en ligne	rabbit	le lapin
mechanic	le/la mécanicien(ne)	open (v)	ouvrir	radio	la radio
medal	la médaille	opinion	l'avis (m)	rain (v)	pleuvoir
medium height	de taille moyenne	or	ou	rap	le rap
meet (v)	rencontrer	orchestra	l'orchestre (m)	read (v)	lire
meet (v) up with	retrouver	organic (adj)	bio	reading	la lecture
melody	la mélodie	organise (v)	organiser	really	vraiment
melon	le melon	original (adj)	original(e)	receive (v)	recevoir
member	le membre	others	les autres (m.pl)	recently	récemment
message	le message			recycle (v)	recycler
midday	midi			recycling	le centre de
middle-sized	de taille moyenne			centre	recyclage

P

mid-length (adj)	mi-long(ue)			red (adj)	rouge
milk	le lait	paper	le papier	reduce (v)	réduire
milk products	les produits (m.pl)	park	le parc	refuse (v)	refuser
	laitiers	participate	participer (v) (à)	reggae	le reggae
modern (adj)	moderne	(v) (in)		region	la région
Monday	lundi	particularly	tellement	remain (v)	rester
money	l'argent (m)	part-time job	le petit boulot	respect (v)	respecter
monument	le monument	party	la fête	rest (v)	se reposer
moon	la Lune	passport	le passeport	restaurant	le restaurant/resto
more	plus	patient (adj)	patient(e)	reuseable (adj)	réutilisable
morning	le matin	PE	l'EPS (f)	rhythm	le rythme
most (of)	la plupart de	perhaps	peut-être	rice	le riz
mother	la mère	phone	le portable	rich (adj)	riche
mountain	la montagne	photo	la photo	right, on the	à droite
museum	le musée (d'art)	piano	le piano	right, to be (v)	avoir (v) raison
(of art)		pick (v) (up)	ramasser	river	la rivière
musician	le/la musicien(ne)	picture	l'image (f)	romantic	romantique
music	la musique	pilot	le/la pilote	rubbish (adj)	nul(le)
mysterious (adj)	mystérieux(–se)	pink (adj)	rose	rubbish	les déchets (m.pl)
		pizza	la pizza	rugby	le rugby
		planet	la planète		

N

S

		plans	les projets (m.pl)		
		plastic	le plastique		
		plastic (adj)	en plastique		
national (adj)	national(e)	play (v)	jouer (v) (à / de)	salad	la salade
naughty (adj)	méchant(e)	police officer	le/la policier(–ère)	Saturday	samedi
		pollute (v)	polluer	savings	les économies (f.pl)
		popcorn	le popcorn	say (v)	dire

Glossaire (anglais – français)

Glossa

Vert/Rou

science	les sciences *(f.pl)*
scientist	le/la scientifique
sea	la mer
sea *(adj)*	marin(e)
secondary school	le collège
see *(v)*	voir
selfie	le selfie
Senegal	le Sénégal
sense of humour	le sens de l'humour
Seychelles	les Seychelles *(f.pl)*
shirt	la chemise
shoe	la chaussure
shop	le magasin
shopping centre	le centre commercial
short *(adj)*	court(e)
shy *(adj)*	timide
simple *(adj)*	simple
since	depuis
sing *(v)*	chanter
singer	le/la chanteur(–se)
single-use	à usage unique
sister	la sœur
site	le site
situated *(adj)*	situé(e)
sixth form (college)	le lycée
skirt	la jupe
sleep *(v)*	dormir
small *(adj)*	petit(e)
snowboarding	le snowboard
sock	la chaussette
something	quelque chose
sometimes	parfois
song	la chanson
south	le sud
South America	l'Amérique *(f)* du Sud
souvenir	le souvenir
Spain	l'Espagne *(f)*
speak	parler
spend *(v)* time with	passer *(v)* du temps avec
spider	l'araignée *(f)*
sport	le sport
stadium	le stade
start *(v)*	commencer
stay (remain) *(v)*	rester
stay *(v)*	loger
stop *(v)*	arrêter
strawberry	la fraise
strict *(adj)*	sévère
study *(v)*	étudier
stupid *(adj)*	bête
subject	la matière
subscriber	l'abonné *(m)*
success	le succès
suit	le costume
summer	l'été
sunbathe *(v)*	se bronzer
Sunday	dimanche
sunset	le coucher du soleil
super *(adj)*	super
supermarket	le supermarché

surf *(v)*	surfer
surfer	le/la surfeur(–se)
sweatshirt	le sweat
sweet	le bonbon
swim *(v)*	nager
swimming pool	la piscine
Switzerland	la Suisse

T

take *(v)*	prendre
tall *(adj)*	grand(e)
tasty *(adj)*	savoureux(–se)
teacher	le professeur
teacher, primary school	l'instituteur(–rice)
team	l'équipe
techno music	la techno
ten	dix
than	que/qu'
that; it	ça
theatre	le théâtre
then	puis
there is/are	il y a
there was/were	il y avait
there will be	il y aura
thing	la chose
think *(v)*	penser
ticket	le billet
tidy *(v)* (up)	ranger
tie	la cravate
tiger	le tigre
time	le temps
time (une fois= one time/ once)	la fois
timetable	l'emploi *(m)* du temps
tiring *(adj)*	fatigant(e)
today	aujourd'hui
together	ensemble
tomorrow (evening)	demain (soir)
too	trop
tortoise	la tortue
(world) tour	le tour (du monde)
tourist	le/la touriste
tower	la tour
town	la ville
train *(v)*	s'entraîner
trainers	les baskets *(f.pl)*
training	la formation
travel *(v)*	voyager
trousers	le pantalon
trumpet	la trompette
try *(v)* (to)	essayer *(v)* (de)
tune	la mélodie
Tunisia	la Tunisie
two (times/ twice)	deux (fois)

U

ugly *(adj)*	laid(e)
unique *(adj)*	unique

United States	les États-Unis *(m.pl)*
university	l'université *(f)*
use *(v)*	utiliser
useful *(adj)*	utile

V

varied *(adj)*	varié(e)
vegetable	le légume
vegetarian *(adj)*	végétarien(ne)
vegetarianism	le végétarisme
very	très
vet	le/la vétérinaire
video clip(s)	le(s) clip(s) vidéo
video game(s)	le jeu(x) vidéo
view	la vue
village	le village
violin	le violon
virtual *(adj)*	virtuel(le)
(guided) visit	la visite (guidée)
visit *(v)*	visiter
voluntary *(adj)*	bénévole
vulnerable *(adj)*	vulnérable

W

walk	la promenade
wash *(v)*	laver
washing-up	la vaisselle
watch *(v)*	regarder
water	l'eau *(f)*
water park	le parc aquatique
wear *(v)*	porter
weather	le temps
website	le site web
Wednesday	mercredi
week	la semaine
weekend	le weekend
well	bien
west	l'ouest *(m)*
what	que/qu'
when	quand
where	où
white *(adj)*	blanc(he)
who	qui
why	pourquoi
wife	la femme
win *(v)*	gagner
with (whom)	avec (qui)
without	sans
woman	la femme
work	le travail; le boulot
work *(v)*	travailler
world	le monde
write *(v)*	écrire
wrong, to be *(v)*	avoir *(v)* tort

Y

year	l'an *(m)*; l'année *(f)*
yellow *(adj)*	jaune
yesterday	hier
young *(adj)*	jeune
young person	le/la jeune

Dynamo 3 © Pearson Education Ltd 2020